FOLK LEGACIES REVISITED

FOLK LEGACIES
REVISITED

David Steven Cohen

Rutgers University Press
New Brunswick, New Jersey

Library of Congress Cataloging-in-Publication Data

Cohen, David Steven, 1943–
    Folk legacies revisited / by David Steven Cohen.
        p.   cm.
    Includes bibliographical references and index.
    ISBN 0-8135-2138-6 (cloth)—ISBN 0-8135-2139-4 (pbk.)
        1. Folklore—New Jersey. 2. Folklore—New York. 3. Ethnicity—
    United States. 4. New Jersey—Social life and customs. 5. New
    York—Social life and customs. I. Title.
    GR110.N5C63   1995
    398'.09749—dc20   94-16185
                                                              CIP

British Cataloging-in-Publication information available.

Lines from William Carlos Williams's "To Elsie," from his *Collected Poems, 1909–1939*, vol. 1, copyright 1938 by New Directions Publishing Company, are reprinted by permission of New Directions.

For my daughter
Alicia Gabrielle Cohen

CONTENTS

ACKNOWLEDGMENTS

ome of the chapters in this book were originally published as articles in history and folklore journals. Some were presented as papers at academic conferences. I have brought them together because there is an underlying theme that runs through them that has relevance to some important issues facing America today, and their collection in a single volume will bring these essays to a larger audience.

Chapter 1, on emergent Native American groups in New Jersey, originated as a paper delivered at the Fortieth Annual International Congress of Americanists in Stockholm and Uppsala, Sweden, July 4–9, 1994.

Chapter 2, on Afro-Dutch folklore and folklife, was presented in 1984 at the annual Rensselaerswyck Seminar in Albany. It was published, along with the other papers presented at that conference, in the *Journal of the Afro-American Historical and Genealogical Society*. I wish to thank Charles Gehring of the New Netherland Project for his invitation to deliver the paper and the editors of the above-mentioned journal for their permission to reprint it. Marilyn M. White of Kean College read this essay and made constructive and thoughtful suggestions for improving it.

Chapter 3, on the origin of the "Pineys," was researched and written as the New Jersey Historical Commission's contribution to the

Pinelands Folklife Project conducted in 1983 by the American Folklife Center of the Library of Congress. It was published in 1985 in the Library of Congress's *Folklife Annual*. David Fowler of the David Library of the American Revolution gave me helpful leads on sources concerning Joseph Mulliner and William Giberson. Howard Green, research director at the New Jersey Historical Commission, made useful comments and suggestions. Alan Jabbour and James Hardin of the American Folklife Center provided editorial assistance.

Chapter 4, on the "Angel Dancers," was originally presented at the American Folklore Society convention in 1976 and published in 1977 in *New Jersey History*. I wish to thank Robert Burnett, formerly of the New Jersey Historical Society, for locating the visuals that accompanied the article.

The final chapter on the significance of ethnicity in American history was presented in 1991 as the Alexander C. Flick lecture at the annual conference on New York State History at Bard College. It was originally published in *New York History*. I thank Stefan Bielinski, director of the Colonial Albany Social History Project, for suggesting the idea of this lecture and Wendell E. Tripp, Jr. of the New York State Historical Association for his editorial advice as I was preparing it for publication.

Finally, I wish to thank Marlie Wasserman, formerly editor in chief at Rutgers University Press, who insisted that these essays constitute a coherent book; Marilyn Campbell, managing editor at the press, who gently yet firmly moved the manuscript through the production process; Victoria Wilson-Schwartz, who copyedited the manuscript in a thorough and thoughtful manner; and my wife, Linda Prentice Cohen, who helped me read the page proofs.

FOLK LEGACIES REVISITED

We have a few old mouth-to-mouth tales; we exhume from old trunks and boxes and drawers letters without salutation or signature, in which men and women who once lived and breathed now merely initials or nicknames out of some now incomprehensible affection which sound to us like Sanskrit or Chocktaw; we see dimly people, the people in whose living blood and seed we ourselves lay dormant and waiting, in this shadowy attenuation of time possessing now heroic proportions, performing their acts of simple passion and simple violence, impervious to time and inexplicable—

William Faulkner,
Absalom, Absalom!

INTRODUCTION

on-folklorists are fond of announcing the demise of folklore. "The period 1870–1930 . . . was the last in which America had a widespread, vital and self-sufficient pattern of folk culture that expressed itself in the visual arts," wrote art historian Robert Hughes in his book about Amish quilts.

Folk art went because folk went. Part of America, old America, the primitive republic of independence and self-help, was disappearing, and its records had to be kept. Its forms would very soon be diluted and destroyed—and then "revived" as tourist emblems of nostalgic images—by the inexorable pressures of the late nineteenth and early twentieth century.

Mass production meant buying things ready-made, first from peddlers and then at stores, instead of making them oneself. Isolated farms and whole hamlets found themselves drawn into the mainstream by traveling salesmen, cars, phones, radio and the impact of the common imagery of the movies. Clans could no longer hold together; the pull of the larger community was too great.

Hughes created an idealized world of the self-sufficient, isolated folk, embodied in "the unfussed refinement of good Shaker furniture—a refinement that rises from practical economy disciplined by the literal belief that God, in Mies van der Rohe's phrase, is in the details."[1] He romanticized the folk only to dismiss them as not measuring up to his romanticized notion of them. This does an injustice to the folk by distorting who they are and how they are perceived. The present study offers a very different notion of the relationship between folklore and history, one that sees both as having a continuing relevance to today's world.

While they were written at different times and under different circumstances, the essays in this book have something in common. They all deal in one way or another with the formation of group identity out of shared folklore, including the folklore of the group's origins (which may or may not be entirely consistent with ascertainable historical fact). The essays concern different kinds of groups—racial, regional, religious, and ethnic—yet for each an understanding of the group's folklore, in the context of its history, is integral to comprehending the identity of the group and its relationship to American society.

The groups I shall discuss are located in New York and New Jersey, but they tell us something about America in general. Each group has been stigmatized at one time or another as impure or, in related terms, as inbred, degenerate, bogus, fanatical, unwholesome, foreign, or un-American. Is there such a thing as cultural purity? Who defines what is American and what is not? These groups may all be what was once called "marginal," but as some scholars have noted, what occurs on the boundaries of a culture contributes to an understanding of its essential identity.[2] As we explore the history and folklore of these groups, their relationship to American culture as a whole will be illuminated.

Chapter 1 is about the complicated web of history and legend surrounding three emergent Native-American groups in New Jersey. I refer to these groups as "emergent" because it is only recently, that is, in the past ten years, that they have organized themselves into tribes. The issue of their status as tribes is complicated by a touchier one—that of "miscegenation"—for many individuals in these groups have black ancestry. In fact, many African Americans have some Indian ancestry, but few set themselves apart on this basis or attempt to organize themselves into an Indian tribe. What makes the issue so complicated is that there are several groups in the eastern United States that can trace their ancestry to known Indian tribes, but because of intermarriage with blacks they were detribalized by a white society that viewed any amount of black ancestry as defining a person as black. In other cases, the tribe was disbanded in order to privately sell its land. Today, controversies over any group's claim to tribal status are heightened by a 1988 federal law that entitles Indian tribes recognized by the federal government to run legal gambling operations if gambling is allowed anywhere else in the state. This makes the stakes very large in New Jersey, where gambling has been legal in Atlantic City since 1976.

Chapter 2 is about another racial group, in this case a regional variant of African-American culture that I term Afro-Dutch. This culture flourished in the Dutch settled regions of New York and New Jersey from the seventeenth through the early twentieth centuries. While the subculture has faded away, one still finds black families with Dutch surnames in this region. Afro-Dutch culture was creole in character; that is, it was a New World creation that combined African cultural survivals with adaptations of European culture. Its distinctive characteristics can be seen in language, folk belief, material culture, and customs, most notably the Afro-Dutch celebration of Pinkster, which commemorates the appearance of the Holy Ghost to the disciples after Jesus' crucifixion. In its folk manifestation it became a carnival celebration similar to those in the Caribbean, South America, and New Orleans. It was folk traditions such as this that defined the cultural identity of the Afro-Dutch.

The so-called "Pineys" of the Pine Barrens in southern New Jersey are yet another kind of group. They constitute a group more defined by region than by race, that lives in a sparsely populated part of the state. Contrary to popular misconception, this region was never as isolated as it was depicted. It was the site of early sawmills, iron mining, glass blowing, and later cranberry and blueberry cultivation. The region is perhaps best known nationwide through John McPhee's book *The Pine Barrens,* which first appeared as an article in the *New Yorker* in 1967.[3] But McPhee and others who have written about the "Pineys" have been caught up in a folk legend about their origins which conveys a highly negative group stereotype. In his work, as so often elsewhere, the people of the Pinelands are portrayed as the inbred, degenerate descendants of disaffected Quakers; pirates, privateers, and smugglers; Hessian soldiers who fought as mercenaries for the British during the Revolutionary War; so-called Pine Robbers who preyed on both sides during the Revolution; Tories, who sided with the British; and remnants of the Lenape Indians who lived on the Brotherton Indian reservation on the outskirts of the Pine Barrens. The genealogical record shows that while parts of this legend contain the proverbial kernel of truth, most of it has no foundation other than the fear and contempt with which some people regard those who live on the margins of society. The region is now undergoing a redefinition of its image: it was designated a "national reserve" in 1978, with a resulting name change from the Pine Barrens to the Pinelands.

The news coverage of the tragic attack in the spring of 1993 on the Branch Davidian complex in Waco, Texas, by officials of the Bureau of Alcohol, Tobacco, and Firearms and the Federal Bureau of Investigation raises questions about religious cults in America. The distinction between sects and so-called cults is vague, to say the least, and one might say that a "cult" is simply a sect of which one disapproves. Some sects, like the Shakers, have been romanticized and idealized, their historic relationship with the rest of society being distorted in the process. Other sects, like the Puritans, the Quakers, and the Mormons, have become part of the religious establishment in the United States. Still others have been demonized. A small religious sect in Woodcliff, New Jersey, known as the "Angel Dancers," provides some insight into what I have termed the folklore of religious communitarianism. Sects tend to inspire rumors, and these rumors tend to contain the same motifs: that the leaders of the sects declare themselves to be the embodiment of God, that members of the sects are held captive against their wills, and that these sects engage in sexual orgies. In my examination of the rumors circulated about the Angel Dancers, I not only show that they were probably untrue but, more importantly, I note the sanctimonious attitudes revealed when people label a sect a "cult" and the resultant misunderstanding of the relationship between religious sects and American society.

The last chapter in the book is my examination as a folklorist of the significance of ethnicity in American history. I do not try to define ethnicity, just as I do not try to define folklore. The reason is that there is no perfect definition of either term, and when one dares to offer a definition, quibbling over the definition replaces all other discussion. Suffice it to say, as I do in that chapter, that ethnicity is a separate group identity in a pluralistic society that is related to, yet different from, nationality, religion, language, race, kinship, or region. Furthermore, an ethnic group is not necessarily the same as an immigrant group. The latter term usually refers to ethnic groups that emerged in the United States in the nineteenth and twentieth centuries, while I argue that there were already ethnic groups in colonial America, including the English, Scots, Welsh, Dutch, Swedes, Finns, Germans,

French, and Spaniards. Some ethnic groups, such as Native Americans and African Americans, did not come to this country by immigration, unless one includes within that concept the prehistoric migration of the ancestors of Native Americans from Siberia and the forcible importation of slaves from Africa. My thesis is that ethnicity probably has been a more significant factor than the frontier in shaping the local, regional, and national cultures of America, not just in the nineteenth and twentieth centuries, but from the beginning of human settlement in North America.

These essays also have implications for academic advocacy, which has become fashionable in universities today. When my first book, *The Ramapo Mountain People* was published in 1974, I thought of it as a form of "applied folklore," which was the term used then for advocacy. At that time, the Ramapough Indians were known as the "Jackson Whites," and the folklore about them was viciously derogatory. They were viewed by outsiders as an inbred group of "hillbillies" living only forty-five minutes from New York City. Being a naive graduate student, I had hoped that my research proving that they were descendants of free black landowners who were culturally Dutch was preferable to the legend that their ancestors were renegade Indians, escaped slaves, Hessian deserters, and Revolutionary War prostitutes. Even before the book was published I realized that the Ramapo Mountain People themselves preferred their own version of the legendary past, which emphasized Indian and white ancestry, to the documented history of free black heritage. I have always felt that their denial of their free black ancestry was a poignant comment on racial attitudes in America, namely, that being Indian is considered better than being black.

What is more problematic are the anthropologists, folklorists, and historians who take the position that there are no objective historical facts. True, there are epistomological problems in all fields of knowledge, but this does not prevent, or excuse, us from trying to determine whether or not a given statement about the past is supported by documentary evidence. Yet it is no longer in fashion to view history as a methodology that attempts to build interpretations of the past based on documentary evidence. Instead, historical studies at most contemporary universities have become a form of advocacy, as witnessed by the rise of courses that promote the political agendas of specific interest groups: labor studies, women's studies, peace studies, gay and lesbian studies.

There is a parallel tendency in the fields of folklore and anthropology. Anthropologists have taken the side of nontribal native peoples against the Bureau of Indian Affairs, whom they criticize for having an unstated policy of not recognizing new Indian tribes, especially east of the Mississippi River. Perhaps the criteria for tribal recognition used by the BIA are too strict, especially the requirement that the group can prove continuous existence as a tribe since the period of first contact with Europeans. However, there is a great deal at stake in being recognized as a tribe by the BIA. It conveys a unique status, for Indian tribes are considered sovereign legal entities and therefore immune from certain federal and state regulations. It is unfortunate that their zeal as advocates has blinded certain anthropologists to the importance of historical data in distinguishing between different kinds of claims to Indian ancestry.

The advocacy issue is very complex, but surely the notion that one should put advocacy for the group above all other considerations, including that of historical truth, is ill-considered. Twenty years after the publication of *The Ramapo Mountain People,* circumstances have changed drastically. At that time the federal government was embarked upon its War on Poverty and the Ramapo Mountain People qualified for several government aid programs based on their economic need. Today groups qualify for government benefits not because of their need but because of who they are. Ironically, my advocacy for the Ramapo Mountain People twenty years ago, when I attempted to replace the derogatory stereotype of the "Jackson Whites" with the documented history of free black landowners, is today viewed as blocking their aspirations to gain federal recognition as an Indian tribe and thereby qualify for government aid.

Advocacy among folklorists has taken the form of cultural conservation. The intent has been to see traditional culture in the same light as old buildings and natural resources that are worthy of government-sponsored efforts at conservation. These folklorists distinguish between preservation and conservation. Preservation is freezing a tradition that is no longer subject to the dynamic changes that living cultures undergo; conservation is the attempt by members of a group (assisted by the advocate-folklorist) to keep their traditions from dying out.[4] However, folklorists who adhere to this concept have taken sides in disputes that pit traditional groups—such as Native Americans, loggers, and cowboys—against environmentalists. In the New Jersey Pinelands folklorists have sometimes sided with local interest groups, including farmers, cranberry and blueberry growers, and other landowners, against the regulations of the Pinelands Commission, established by the state of New Jersey in 1979 to protect the environment.[5] These regulations have adversely affected property values, and residents are understandably upset. But the regulations were designed to fend off the overdevelopment that, in the long run, destroys not only the natural environment but the traditional cultures it nourishes.

The effort to change the stereotype of the Pineys as degenerate outcasts to a more positive image as stewards of the landscape has dangerous implications. Folklore can be used by folklorists to idealize the folk, to celebrate their lives as somehow purer than ours. Then folklore is being used to manipulate political images, and the homage paid to so-called community and family values becomes a mask for political and economic self-interest. In fact, there are all kinds of conflicting interests in the Pinelands, sometimes even putting different traditional activities at odds with each other. For example, drawing off the fresh water from the Cohansey aquifer for use in irrigating farmlands increases the salinity in the freshwater marshes along the rivers, which endangers the habitat for the traditional activity of railbird shooting. The free-flowing waters that are desirable to cranberry growers to wet-harvest their crop are anathema to the cedar loggers, who need obstructed streams to create the swamp habitat in which cedar grows.

The romantic idealization of some folk groups and the demonization of others is what highly charged terms like "cult" represent for American religious groups. Religion is based on belief, which is one of the subjects that folklorists study, but few people seem to accept the power of belief as a historical force. For example, I have argued elsewhere that historians have failed to understand the Salem witchcraft trials, because they have not recognized the simple fact that the Puritans believed in witches. Because few historians have asked themselves how a sincere belief in the existence of witches might influence individual and communal behavior, they have tried to find other explanations of the trials, such as persecution of women, outsiders, or minorities.[6] In my discussion of the "Angel Dancers," I am not attempting to deny that there have been religious leaders who have misled their followers or who have had undue influence over them. My point, rather, is that religious belief has been a strong force in America throughout its history, and that it is too convenient to dismiss those religious sects with which we don't agree as "cults" at the same time that we glorify others, like the Shakers, the Puritans, and the Quakers.

While it may seem that I am taking contradictory positions in reference to the Pineys and the Angel Dancers, cautioning against advocacy in the case of the former and embracing the cause of the latter, I do not think this is true. In using historical and genealogical research to refute the negative stereotype implied in the legend about the origins of the Pineys, I am being an advocate for them too. What I oppose is the kind of advocacy that puts loyalty to the group above all else, including historical fact.

Multiculturalism is another area where advocacy has blurred our vision. In large part ethnic studies in recent years has aimed at instilling group pride and/or furthering a political agenda. This is in my opinion unfortunate, because it has hurt the cause of multiculturalism.[7] We should recognize the contributions of each ethnic group to the shaping of American culture not in order to instill pride in the members of that group but in order to better understand what American culture is and how it came to be. The debate is between those who believe that American culture is predominantly Anglo-American, because our political institutions and language derive from England, versus those who, while acknowledging the English contribution, have a broader vision of American life, one which includes, among other things, foodways, slang, music, dance, and material culture.

The Afro-Dutch culture in New York and New Jersey is a case in point. My focus is not on the contributions of great men and women, that is, on culture heroes, or even on the making of a national African American culture.[8] I am concerned here with the cultural dynamics at work in the creation of a regional African American culture that was distinctly creole in character. It combined African survivals with cultural borrowings from the dominant Dutch Americans in the region. While the influence of Afro-Dutch culture did not extend beyond its regional boundaries, it was nevertheless a part of American culture by virtue of being a regional subculture. This is sufficient significance. There is no need to make exaggerated claims, like those who argue that American democracy was inspired by the Iroquois Confederacy in the face of evidence that the Founding Fathers were clearly thinking of Greek and Roman models of government. It is sufficient to point out that American culture is different from European culture and that the difference stems in large part from the presence of African Americans and Native Americans on this continent.

In recent years there has been a strong upsurge of anti-immigrant sentiment. Many blamed the severe recession of the early 1990s on illegal aliens, and laws were passed declaring English to be the official language of the land. Like earlier periods of xenophobia, recent immigrants are being viewed as foreigners by the children and grandchildren of people who were themselves immigrants. Part of this is a reaction to the Ethnic Revival of the 1970s and 1980s in which white ethnic groups sought to instill the same sense of pride in their members that the Black Power movement instilled in African Americans. There are those, like historian Orlando Patterson, who disapprove of ethnicity, because it has often degenerated into ethnic chauvinism.[9] In some ways ethnic studies have been the best evidence to support Patterson's criticisms. But that's not the point. Whether or not one approves of ethnicity, it will not go away. Unfortunately, the debate about multiculturalism has deteriorated into an argument between the Afrocentrists, who are obsessed with trying to prove that Africans were the first or the best in any given area, versus scholars, like historian Arthur Schlesinger, Jr., who define American culture solely by its language or political institutions and distrust ethnicity as destructive of our national unity.[10]

There are those who relegate ethnic groups, like the other groups in this book, to a marginal status. However, those who define American national character as anything other than the sum of all its diverse parts typically find themselves trading in stereotypes. Those who view

American character in terms of individualism, democracy, or the frontier tend to generalize from their own region or ethnic group. Despite attempts to exclude one or another group from the privileged circle of "true" Americans, in the last analysis we are all, to use the words of poet William Carlos Williams, "the pure products of America."

I

EMERGENT NATIVE AMERICAN GROUPS IN NEW JERSEY

The pure products of America
go crazy—
mountain folk from Kentucky
or the ribbed north end of
Jersey

S o begins William Carlos Williams's poem "To Elsie," which I quoted in my 1974 book *The Ramapo Mountain People.* I noted there that this poem was about one of the racially mixed people, then called the "Jackson Whites," living in the Ramapo Mountains on the New York-New Jersey border, as witnessed by the reference in the poem to "marriage / perhaps / with a dash of Indian blood." At the time I considered the poem to be a reflection of Williams's class and racial prejudices against the mountain people and his willingness to accept uncritically the legends about their origins.

Anthropologist James Clifford changed my thinking about this poem. In his 1988 book *The Predicament of Culture,* Clifford cites the poem as an expression of the plight of native peoples in a modern age.

> Call the predicament ethnographic modernity: eth-nographic because Williams finds himself off center among scattered traditions; modernity since the condition of rootlessness and mobility he confronts is an increasingly common fate. "Elsie" stands simultaneously for a local cultural breakdown and a collective future.

Clifford sees two possibilities: "Elsie is either the last all-but-assimilated remnant of the Tuscaroras who, according to tradition, settled in the Ramapough [*sic*] hills of northern New Jersey, or she represents a Native American past that is being turned into an unexpected future." The unexpected future to which he refers is the fact that over the past decade the Ramapo Mountain People "have actively asserted an Indian identity." Citing my book as "debunking the story of a Tuscarora offshoot," Clifford maintains that "whatever its real historic roots, the tribe as presently constituted is a living impure product."

Clifford's book contains an essay about the 1977 land claims trial in Boston Federal Court of the so-called Mashpee Indians of Cape Cod. He sees the trial as an example of modern Indians having to "convince a white Boston jury of their authenticity." Who has the right to determine who is an Indian and what is authentically Indian? Clifford compares the Mashpee to "several other eastern groups such as the Lumbee and Ramapough" that have intermarried with blacks and were therefore identified in the past by the census takers and other outsiders as "colored." Clifford argues that "twentieth century identities no longer presuppose continuous culture or traditions. Everywhere individuals and groups improvise local performances from (re)collected pasts, drawing in foreign media, symbols, and languages." In other words, the Mashpee, the Ramapough, and other native peoples "reinvented tradition" in the twentieth century. As a modernist poet, Williams, Clifford maintains, intuitively realized there was no such thing as authentic tradition.

> Here, and throughout his writings, Williams avoids pastoral, folkloristic appeals of the sort common among other liberals in the twenties—exhorting, preserving, collecting a true rural culture in endangered places like Appalachia. Such authenticities would be at best artificial aesthetic purifications. . . .
> Let this problematic figure with her "dash of Indian blood," her ungainly female form, her inarticulateness stand for groups marginalized or silenced in the bourgeois West: "natives," women, the poor. . . . She, Williams, all of us are caught in modernity's inescapable momentum.[1]

Although I gained a new understanding of Williams's poem from Clifford's analysis, in this essay I want to take issue with his deconstructionist approach, which views historical facts as irrelevant to the ongoing process of reinvention. Rather than being "artificial aesthetic purifications," history and folklore allow us to make distinctions that Clifford glosses over—distinctions, for example, between groups like the Mashpees who can trace their genealogy to known Indian tribes that intermarried with blacks and groups like the Ramapo Mountain People who, the genealogical record indicates, descend primarily from free blacks and who have only a legendary claim to early Indian ancestry.[2] The importance of such distinctions can be seen in the three emergent Native American groups in New Jersey that have been granted state recognition.

In January 1980, the State of New Jersey passed a concurrent resolution designating the Ramapough (an archaic spelling) Mountain People as the Ramapough Indians and memorializing the Congress of the United States to recognize them as an Indian tribe. The resolution stated that the Ramapo Mountain People "are direct descendants from pure-blooded Indians of the Iroquois and Algonquin [*sic*] nations," thereby broadening the legendary Indian ancestry from Tuscarora (whose language was part of the Iroquoian language family) to include the Lenape or Delaware Indians (the indigenous Indians of New Jersey, whose language has been classified as part of the Algonquian language family). The resolution was forthright in its motivation, indicating that the Ramapo Mountain People were striving for Federal recognition in order to qualify for funds earmarked for Indians. Technically, a resolution such as this is merely a token in that it requests Congress to recognize the group as an Indian tribe; however, the statement attached to the resolution declared that its purpose was for the State of New Jersey also to recognize the mountain people as the Ramapough Indian Tribe.

This resolution was followed later the same year by a bill designating the Powhatan-Renape people as a "nation" (*sic*) and also memorializing Congress to recognize them as a "tribe," and in 1982 a similar resolution was passed for the Confederation of Nanticoke–Lenni Lenape Tribes. These bills, however, unlike the resolution for the Ramapoughs, did not use the term "recognize" either in reference to the state or federal governments. Instead, Congress was memorialized to acknowledge them as tribes. The Powhatan-Renape resolution described the group as "comprised of seven surviving tribes of the Renape linguistic group of the Powhatan alliance or confederation" and noted that "in the nineteenth century many Powhatan Renape People moved to New Jersey." The resolution concerning the Nanticoke–Lenni Lenape describes them as "comprised of several surviving tribes of the Confederation of Nanticoke–Lenni Lenape cultures" and points to "an unbroken history of hundreds of years settlement in the southern New Jersey area." It should be noted that tribes of the Powhatan confederation were indigenous to Virginia and like the Lenape were members of the Algonquian, not the Renape or Lenape, language family. In the Lenape language the *r* and the *l* sounds were interchangeable, according to Columbia University linguist John Dyneley Prince. The term *lenni* means "man" and *lenape* means "people," and current anthropological thinking holds that the use of the terms together is redundant.[3]

The 1990 census lists 14,970 American Indians in New Jersey, yet the Bureau of Indian Affairs in the United States Department of the Interior currently recognizes no tribes in the state. This disparity has several explanations. First, there are individual Native Americans from tribes outside the state who have migrated to New Jersey. Second, since 1970 the census has used self-identification as the rule for determining racial origin. In 1980, 8,394 census respondents in New Jersey identified themselves as Indians; by 1990 this figure had increased by 78.3 percent. This upward trend is part of a national pattern and cannot be explained by in-migration or natural increase alone. A demographer for the Census Bureau told the *New York Times:* "Apparently, people who did not call themselves Indians in an earlier census are now doing so."[4]

Anthropologists have noted that it is not uncommon for ethnic groups to change their identity or for new ethnic identities to emerge. Certainly this has been the case with such groups as the Ukrainians, who have been known at different times in their history as Little Russians or Ruthenians, and only in the twentieth century have been designated Ukrainians. Among American Indians, new tribes have been formed from the remnants of old ones. Such was the case with the Seminoles and the Mashpees. Furthermore, there is no one definition of what constitutes a tribe, and there are often conflicts between legal and anthropological definitions. But the issue we are tackling here is not simply a how to define a tribe. It is necessary to distinguish between a group of people that has existed for some time as a tribe, a group that has so existed at one time, and a group that only recently has taken on a tribal identity.[5]

In my book *The Ramapo Mountain People* I contrasted the legend of their origins to their documented genealogical history. According to legend their ancestors were Tuscarora Indians migrating from North Carolina to New York State in the seventeenth century, escaped slaves, Hessian deserters from the British army during the Revolutionary War, and prostitutes procured by a man named Jackson for the British soldiers occupying New York City during the Revolution. The name Jackson White, according to the legend, came from the fact that some of the women were black, hence "Jackson's Blacks," and others were white, that is, "Jackson's Whites." More likely the name comes from the phrase "jacks and whites," "free jacks" being a slang expression for free blacks.

The genealogical record indicates that the Ramapo Mountain People descend from free blacks who were culturally Dutch, a group I will discuss at length in chapter 2. I traced the oldest families back to the late seventeenth century to a community of free blacks living on the outskirts of New York City. In 1687, three of these families were the original patentees in the Tappan Patent in the Hackensack Valley on the disputed boundary between New York and New Jersey. Throughout the eighteenth century these "colored pioneers" lived in the Hackensack Valley as landowners. At the turn of the nineteenth century, they began to sell their property in the valley and buy land in the Ramapo Mountains. The probable reason for this migration was the passage of a slave code in New Jersey that required free blacks to have a pass to cross state or county boundaries. Since the boundary line between New York and New Jersey had been run through the

distant from Lewes, which she owned and carried on herself. . . . Her name she gave as Regua, and she was childless, but whether maid or widow, or a wife astray, she never disclosed to anyone. . . . After she had been living in Angola Neck quite a number of years, a slaver was driven into Lewes Creek. . . .

Miss or Mrs. Regua, having heard of the presence of the slaver in the harbor, and having lost one of her men slaves, went to Lewes, and to replace him, purchased another from the slave ship. She selected a very tall, shapely and muscular young fellow of dark ginger-bread color, who claimed to be a prince or chief of one of the tribes of the Congo River. . . . This young man had been living with his mistress but a few months when they were duly married, and as Lydia told the court and the jury, they reared quite a large family of children, who as they grew up were not permitted to associate and intermarry with their neighbors of pure Caucasian blood, nor were they disposed to seek associations or alliance with the Negro race; so that they were so necessarily compelled to associate and intermarry with the remnant of the Nanticoke tribe of Indians who still lingered in their old habitations for many years after the great body of the tribe had been removed further towards the setting sun.[16]

On the basis of this testimony, Sockum was convicted of selling powder and shot to a mulatto, and after the trial he closed his store and moved to Gloucester, New Jersey. Weslager cites a local historian who believes that the Ridgeway family are the descendants of Regua and the Congo slave. Speck reported that in 1865 some members of the Harmon family moved to Blackwood Town, New Jersey.[17]

The Nanticokes, a tribe known from historical documents, re-sided on the Chesapeake Bay side of the Delmarva Peninsula. There was a tradition among them that they were once part of the Lenape, but anthropologists today think that they were culturally distinct.[18] In the 1740s, under the pressure of European encroachment, most of the Nanticoke left the Delmarva Peninsula, first seeking the protection of the Iroquois in the Susquehanna Valley of Pennsylvania and finally settling on a reservation in Ontario, Canada. Some, however, remained in Delaware and intermarried with blacks. As one indication that not all the Indians left Delaware, Weslager notes the fact that in the 1790s a woman named Weningominsk, whose European name was Mary Mulberry, was the leader of the Choptank Indians residing at Locust Neck. Furthermore, Weslager cites two surnames extant among the Indian River Nanticoke in Delaware that were associated with the original tribe: Coursey and Street. An Indian named John Coursey was one of the signators of a 1742 treaty, and the surname Street occurs both among the Nanticoke descendants in Canada and in Delaware.[19]

Thus, unlike the Ramapough Indians, whose claim to early In-dian ancestry is unsupported by historical evidence, there is genea-logical evidence of some early Indian ancestry for the present-day Nanticokes of Delaware. However, this Indian connection is limited to only one or two individual ancestors. The evidence for the Indian ancestry of the so-called Nanticoke–Lenni Lenape in New Jersey is even more tenuous. It stems from some Delaware Nanticokes who moved to New Jersey and intermarried with individuals from the free black community of Gouldtown outside of Bridgeton. There is a legend of Lenape ancestry in at least one of the Gouldtown families, but no reliable documentation supports it.

The Powhatan-Renape represent yet a third situation. The "Powhatan Indians" is a collective term for the Algonquian-speaking chiefdoms of Virginia's coastal plain. The name Powhatan refers both to one of the chiefdoms and to its leader at the time of the English settlement. Powhatan, who was the father of Pocahontas, inherited six of these chiefdoms (the Powhatan, Arrohateck, Appamattuck, Pamunkey, Mattaponi, and Chiskiack) and then acquired more, creating what one scholar has described as more an empire than a confederacy. This empire was short-lived, however, breaking apart after a war with the English in the mid-1640s. Unlike the Indians in New Jersey and the northern Delmarva Peninsula, the Indians of Virginia's coastal plain and eastern shore (the lower Delmarva) did not migrate, but they broke up into smaller and smaller groups, occupying smaller and smaller territories. They also began to intermarry with blacks. In 1785, in his *Notes on the State of Virginia,* Thomas Jefferson described the state of the remaining Powhatan groups as follows:

> The *Chickahominies* removed about the year 1661, to Mattapony river. Their chief, with one from each of the Pamunkies and Mattaponies, attended the treaty of Albany in 1685. This seems to have been the last chapter in their history. They retained, however, their separate name so late as 1705, and were at length blended with the Pamunkies and Mattaponies, and exist at present only under their name. There remain of the *Mattaponies* three or four men only, and have more negro than Indian blood in them. They have lost their language, have reduced themselves, by voluntary sales, to about fifty acres of land, which lie on the river of their own name, and have from time to time, been joining the Pamunkies, from whom they are distant but ten miles. The *Pamunkies* are reduced to about ten or twelve men, tolerably pure from mixture with other colors. The older ones among them preserve their language in a small degree, which are the last vestiges on earth, as far as

we know, of the Powhatan language. They have about three hundred acres of very fertile land, on Pamunkey river. . . . Of the *Nottoways,* not a male is left. A few women constitute the remains of that tribe. . . . At a very early period, certain lands were marked out and appropriated to these tribes, and were kept from encroachment by the authority of the laws. They have usually had trustees appointed, whose duty was to watch over their interests, and guard them from insult and injury.[20]

But the trustees did not "watch over their interests" very well, for in the early nineteenth century they participated in the actions on the part of the state of Virginia to dissolve the reservations and detribalize the Indian inhabitants, on the grounds that the Indians had intermarried with free blacks, who were feared as potential inciters of slave insurrections. The termination of tribal status was reinforced by the developing racial attitudes in white Virginia: any amount of black ancestry qualified a person as black.[21]

The New Jersey Powhatan-Renape acknowledge that the Powhatan Indians were located primarily in Virginia, but they claim that some of their number migrated to New Jersey in the eighteenth century. Their current leader, Chief Roy Crazy Horse, wrote in his *A Brief History of the Powhatan Renape Nation:* "The majority of our people are still concentrated in the tidewater region of Virginia, although a sizable population (approximately 1,200) survives in the Delaware Valley region as a result of a migration to the North in the 1700's to escape racism and in search of jobs." There is, however, no historical documentation for this migration. Chief Crazy Horse explains the Powhatan-Renape name as follows:

In ancient times we called ourselves Renape (human beings—the people—our people). Renape has the same meaning and origin as Lenape, the name originally known by the Delaware people. The letter *L* gradually replaced *R* in the Lenni Lenape language. All these people were not united in one tribe. There were many independent republics. Sometimes they came together in alliances or confederations. So Powhatan refers to a political alliance, while Renape refers to an ethnic group—a people speaking a common language.[22]

In 1983 his group reached an agreement with the state of New Jersey for the use of a part of Rancocas State Park in Burlington County, where they have reconstructed an Indian village and museum. Thus, the Powhatan-Renape claim to be descended not from a remnant group left behind when the main group migrated elsewhere but from individuals who migrated to New Jersey after the main group was detribalized because of intermarriage with blacks.

During the 1920s the Powhatan Indians in Virginia and the Nanticoke in Delaware underwent a revitalization under the influence of University of Pennsylvania anthropologist Frank G. Speck. A crisis in Virginia was precipitated when in 1924 the state legislature passed its Racial Integrity Law, requiring the listing of racial ancestry on certificates issued by the state Bureau of Vital Statistics. Speck, who was working on a book about the Rappahannocks and another about the Powhatan tribes, actively helped the racially mixed Indians in Virginia fight the arbitrary designation of them as black. He also encouraged them to revitalize their crafts. Under his guidance, a new Powhatan Confederacy was formed and intertribal gatherings took place, but the effort at renewal was short-lived.[23]

Beginning in 1911, Speck also visited the Nanticoke Indians at the Indian River Hundred. He was instrumental in the incorporation of the Nanticoke Indian Association of Delaware in 1922 and actively encouraged the revitalization of Indian culture in the area. According to Weslager:

> In a further effort to sharpen interest in old Indian traditions, the Association voted to hold an annual festival at Thanksgiving, reminiscent of native campfire pow-wows. Under the guidance of their benefactor, Dr. Speck, they made costumes, strings of beads, and feather head-dresses. He taught them the steps of simple Indian dances and the words to Indian songs. There was no intent to hold up these things as direct survivals of their Nanticoke Indian forebears.[24]

Later, Weslager defended Speck's actions in becoming an advocate for the people he studied:

> One might question the appropriateness of Speck directly involving himself in the process of change of his study group. He may have been one of the first anthropologists studying the Indians east of the Mississippi to become so involved, but participant intervention has recently become more common. In this nontraditional method, the investigator becomes a vital part in the process he is studying while it is taking place. Be that as it may, Speck did not consider the songs and dances as direct survivals handed down from ancient Nanticoke Indian forebears. Speck, as well as the Indians themselves, knew that the original Nanticoke ceremonies, like the native language, had not been preserved.[25]

In the 1970s and 1980s, as part of what has been termed the Ethnic Revival, another movement to revitalize Indian traditions got under way, this time among the emergent Indian groups in New Jersey: the Ramapough, the Nanticoke-Renape, and the Powhatan-Renape. The Powhatan-Renape especially have been effective in obtaining funds from the state arts council for many of their activities. These groups tapped into a growing powwow movement among tribal Indians, nontribal Indians, and non-Indians across the country. The presentation of Indian culture was pan-Indian, that is, a composite of Indian traditions from many different parts of the country. While there are some that may question the "authenticity" of these powwows and see in them a syncretistic stereotype of Indian culture, the fact remains that many Indians have participated in them, and similar composite cultural identities have been formed among other ethnic groups.[26]

The stakes in the cultural politics of obtaining tribal recognition from the federal Bureau of Indian Affairs were increased tremendously in 1988, when the Indian Gaming Act was passed. This act allowed tribes recognized by the BIA to run gambling operations if the state allows such gambling for any other group. However, to be recognized by the BIA the group must prove continuous existence as a tribe, which is difficult to define and, for the groups under discussion, hard to prove. This law has been especially controversial in New Jersey, where casino gambling has been legal in Atlantic City since 1976. In November 1993 the Bureau of Indian Affairs recommended to the secretary of the interior that the Ramapoughs' petition for recognition be denied because they did not meet the criteria established by the BIA, most importantly, continuous existence as a tribe. The ruling was hailed by some members of the New Jersey Congressional delegation, some newspapers, and Donald Trump as a victory for Atlantic City. Trump, the owner of several Atlantic City casinos, suggested that the only reason the Ramapoughs sought Indian recognition was to gain a casino permit. But in fairness to the Ramapoughs, it should be noted that their application for recognition antedated the Indian Gaming Law by eight years.

I believe that it is a mistake to view the Ramapoughs' assertion of Indian identity and that of the other emergent Indian groups in New Jersey as a cynical attempt to gain economic advantages through bogus claims to tribal status. Most of the members of these groups honestly believe that their claims are valid. This is a conflict between different ways of understanding the past: one through the oral tradition of a community; the other through historical research. The two are often difficult to reconcile. The Ramapough Indians understandably put more stock in what they have been told by their parents and grand-parents than in the scholarly footnotes of an outsider.

Certainly, there are difficulties in determining the legal definition of a tribe. Perhaps it is arbitrary for the Bureau of Indian Affairs to stipulate continuous existence as a tribe as the requirement for federal recognition. Very few folk traditions survive within a group in a continuous line from the distant past; most have been revitalized and reinvented. Notwithstanding all this, there is still a need to keep the historical record separate from oral tradition and to make distinctions between different kinds of emergent Native American groups. Otherwise, we are unwittingly providing a new meaning to the closing lines of William Carlos Williams's poem:

> It is only in isolate flocks that
> something
> is given off
> No one
> to witness
> and adjust, no one to drive the car.

2

AFRO-DUTCH FOLKLORE AND FOLKLIFE

n 1862, in the midst of the nation's Civil War, Thomas F. De Voe described the activities of northern slaves at Catherine Market in New York City during the early decades of the nineteenth century. The first introduction in this city of public "negro dancing" no doubt took place in this market. The negroes who visited here were principally slaves from Long Island, who had leave of their masters for certain holidays, among which "Pinkster" was the principal one when, for "pocket money," they would gather up everything that would bring a few pence or shillings, such as roots, berries, herbs, yellow or other birds, fish, clams, oysters, etc., and bring them with them in their skiffs to market; then, as they had usually three days holiday, they were ever ready by their "negro sayings or doings," to make a few shillings more.

The slaves would hire themselves out to engage in a "jig" or "breakdown." Their dancing would be confined to a wooden board, which they called a "shingle." The rhythm was supplied by beating their hands against their legs and by tapping their heels. Sometimes they would dance off the board, which was termed "turning around and shying off." A hat was passed around for each dancer, with the best dancer getting the most money. "Among the most famous in their day," noted De Voe, "was 'Ned' (Francis), a little wiry negro slave, belonging to Martin Ryerson; another named Bob Rowley, who called himself 'Bobolink Bob,' belonging to William Bennett; and Jack, belonging to Frederick De Voo [sic], all farmers on Long Island." Many New Jersey blacks, most from Tappan, would join the dancing at Catharine Market after disposing of their masters' produce at Bear Market.[1] De Voe's memoir is a verbal snapshot of a little-known African-American subculture that developed in the Dutch settlements of New York and New Jersey.

Despite the fact that the Dutch played a central role in the seventeenth-century slave trade, little attention has been paid until recently to the Dutch-owned slaves in New York and New Jersey. Most studies of slavery in the Americas have dealt with the Caribbean, South America, and the southern United States. Few scholars have tested whether conclusions developed from these other areas hold true for New York and New Jersey. Only recently have scholars used folklore as a source of information about the culture of slaves in general. The problem with most interpretations of the Dutch slave system is that they deal only with the New Netherland period (1624–1664).[2] The Dutch and their slaves did not disappear after the English conquest. In fact, the institution of slavery did not begin to flourish in New York and New Jersey until the eighteenth century.

Although, after 1664, English law applied to all inhabitants of the region, it is a mistake to think of the Dutch and their slaves as part of an English slave system. There is evidence in their folklore and

1. Chief Roy Crazy Horse and Powhatan-Renape women at a Native American fashion show, Rancocas State Park, 1985. Courtesy of New Jersey Newsphotos.

2. Tina (Little Flower) Pierce, displaying Indian crafts for sale at the Nanticoke Lenni-Lenape Cultural Center, Bridgeton. Courtesy of New Jersey Newsphotos.

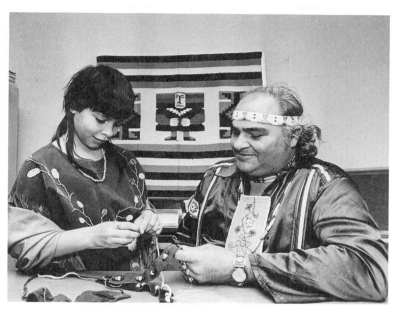

3. Lou Pierce (Gray Squirrel) with daughter Kimberly (Little Owl) at the Nanticoke-Lenni Lenape Cultural Center, Bridgeton. Courtesy of New Jersey Newsphotos.

4. New Amsterdam Scene, 1642–1643, showing Afro-Dutch slaves. Courtesy of the I. N. Phelps Stokes Collection, Miriam and Ira D. Wallace Division of Art, Prints and Photographs, New York Public Library, Astor, Lenox, and Tilden Foundations.

5. Cigar store Indian figure, Freehold, New Jersey, attributed to a slave named Job, circa 1815. Courtesy of the New York State Historical Association, Cooperstown.

6. A stereotypical Piney family. Photograph by Harry Dorer. Courtesy of the Newark Public Library.

7. Portrait of Elizabeth S. Kite. Courtesy of Special Collections and Archives, Rutgers University Libraries.

8. Sketch of Mnason T. Huntsman, from the *Bergen Index,* April 27, 1893. Courtesy of the New Jersey Historical Society.

folklife that a distinct free black and slave culture developed in the Dutch culture area of New York and New Jersey. This regional creole culture consisted of a synthesis of African cultural survivals with Dutch culture traits, and the people who participated in it I term Afro-Dutch. The Afro-Dutch way of life was a regional variant of the African American culture of the United States. But as a creole culture it had much in common with African-derived traditions of South America and the Caribbean.

Although their numbers were relatively small, the Afro-Dutch were culturally significant. The Dutch were the major slaveholders in New York and New Jersey. In 1660 the black population of New York was only about 600. By 1700 it had grown to an estimated 2,256, and by the second decade of the eighteenth century it had more than doubled (5,700). Between 1750 and 1770 an increase of more than seventy percent brought the total to 19,000, and by 1800 the black population of New York was about 39,000. In East New Jersey, which included the Dutch-settled regions, there were only about 120 blacks in 1680. By 1720 there were 2,581 blacks in the entire province of New Jersey, including both East New Jersey and West New Jersey, which were united as a single colony in 1702. Most blacks were concentrated in East New Jersey, which had about 54 percent of the white population, but a disproportionate 74 percent of the blacks. In heavily Dutch Bergen County the population was almost twenty percent black in the eighteenth century, while in heavily Quaker West New Jersey blacks constituted only 4.5 percent of the population at the time of the American Revolution. By 1810 almost all the blacks in southwestern New Jersey were free, while in north central and northeast New Jersey more blacks were slave than free. Most slaves in New Jersey were scattered on relatively small farms, although a few Barbadian and Dutch landowners had large numbers of slaves. For example, Arendt Schuyler in 1776 owned from fifty to sixty slaves.[3]

It has been argued that the type of slave system in operation, the percentage of the total population that was black, and the percentage of the black population that came directly from Africa themselves are correlated with the degree to which African culture survived among the slaves. Anthropologist Melville Herskovits argued that because there was no plantation system in the North and slaveowning was on a relatively small scale, there was more acculturation to European patterns of behavior and thought in what became the northern United States than anywhere else in the world.[4]

Certainly the number of blacks in proportion to the total population was greater in the Caribbean than in North America and greater in the southern United States than in the northern United States. According to historian John A. Rawley, in 1730 Africans constituted only 14 percent of the total population of the thirteen colonies, but about 80 percent of the total population of the British and French Caribbean. Historian Frank Tannenbaum cited an estimate that the colored population of all the Antilles at the beginning of the nineteenth century was about 83 percent of the total population. By contrast, in 1810 blacks constituted about one-eighth of the population of the United States. But the black population was not distributed evenly. In 1780 four states (Virginia, South Carolina, North Carolina, and Maryland) accounted for 85 percent of the total slaves in the United States, a figure that represents the major portion of the total black population. In that year South Carolina had a black majority; Virginia was two-fifths black, and North Carolina and Maryland were about one-third black. In contrast, in 1790 blacks in New Jersey made up only 7.7 percent of the population; in New York, 7.6 percent.[5]

The places of origin of the black population of New York and New Jersey changed with changes in the slave trade. The Dutch slave trade at first targeted Angola and the Gold Coast, and there was indeed an Angolan presence in New Amsterdam as early as 1623, when Domine Jonas Michaelius wrote that "the Angola slaves are thievish, lazy, and useless trash." Between 1630 and 1654 the Dutch occupied parts of Brazil, and some slaves in New Amsterdam appear to have come from there. In 1647 Captain Johan de Fries issued an authorization to Michiel Jansen "to take care of, and justly treat, in his absence, his free Negroes and Brazilian women." There was also the transshipment of slaves via the Dutch slave depot on Curacao in the West Indies. Between 1659 and 1664 six slave ships arrived in New Amsterdam, all of which came by way of Curacao.[6]

After the English conquest of New Netherland, the source of slaves switched to Madagascar and the West Indies. The Dutch New Yorker Frederick Philipse, for example, was a major slave trader in Madagascar. Nevertheless, in the period from 1701 to 1715 about two-fifths of the slaves brought into New York still came directly from Africa. James G. Lydon estimates that between 1701 and 1774 about 2,800 slaves were imported directly from Africa to New York—a revision upward of the widely cited estimate of Elizabeth Donnan that between 1715 and 1765 only 930 out of the 4,551 slaves imported into New York and New Jersey came directly from Africa. Donnan's data indicates that 20 percent of the slaves came from Africa, whereas Lydon's indicates 43 percent.[7]

Rawley suggests that this upward revision affects Herskovits's contention that acculturation of the slaves was greater in the North than in the South. However, Rawley's own figures indicate that direct importation from Africa was even greater in the South. By his reckoning, 92 percent of Maryland's slaves during the period from 1750 to 1773 had been brought there from Africa. More than four-fifths of the slaves imported into Virginia from 1727 to 1769 came directly from Africa, as did approximately 86 percent of those imported into South Carolina between 1735 and 1769.[8]

But the true test of Herskovits's theory is not the percentage that came from Africa, but the degree of acculturation among blacks in

New York and New Jersey. One index of the acculturation of Dutch-owned slaves was language. According to James B. H. Storms of Park Ridge, New Jersey, one of the last speakers of Jersey Dutch (he died in 1949 at the age of eighty-nine): "Even the colored people, for the most part children of slaves, without any education at all, were proficient in the use of Jersey Dutch and had enough knowledge of English to converse in either."9

In 1910 linguist John Dyneley Prince collected some expressions in Jersey Dutch from William De Freece of Ringwood, New Jersey. De Freece, who was one of the Ramapo Mountain People, a racially mixed population that descend from free blacks who were culturally Dutch (see chapter 1), was seventy-five years old at the time. Prince described De Freece as "an excellent authority on the negro variant of the dialect." Prince's white Dutch informants from Bergen County "characterized many of his [De Freece's] words as distinctly 'nigger,' an interesting circumstance showing that the negro slaves of the old settlers used an idiom tinged with their own peculiarities." The white Dutch called this black variant *nexer dauts,* "Negro Dutch." One such "negroism" was the word *plot,* meaning "foot," which Prince described as a "corruption" of the Holland Dutch *poot* and the Jersey Dutch *pot.* Prince noted that "there is a small colony of old negroes living on the mountain back of Suffern, New York, who still use their own dialect of Jersey Dutch." He was referring to another settlement of Ramapo Mountain People, living on Stag Hill in Mahwah, New Jersey.10

The black variant of Jersey Dutch was neither a pidgin nor a creole. According to the linguist Dell Hymes, "pidgins arise as makeshift adaptations, reduced in structure and use, no one's first language; creoles are pidgins become primary languages." He adds, "Both are marginal, in the circumstances of their origin, and in the attitudes towards them on the part of those who speak one of the languages from which they derive."11 The advertisements for runaway slaves suggest that the black variant of Jersey Dutch was not reduced in structure. In 1741 Philip French of New Brunswick advertised for the return of "a Negro Man named Claus . . . [who] speaks Dutch and good English." In 1766 Cornelius Clopper of Raritan Landing advertised for the return of "a yellowish Negro Fellow named Bill . . . [who] speaks good English and Low Dutch fluently." And in 1780 Lucas Van Beverhoudt from Beverwyck (near Morristown, New Jersey) advertised for the return of "a negro man named JACK . . . [who] speaks broken English and some negro Dutch."[12]

Thus, the black dialect of Dutch spoken in New York and New Jersey differs from the Dutch creoles spoken in the Caribbean and South America. Papiamentu, the creole spoken on the islands of Curacao, Aruba, and Bonaire, is thought to be an outgrowth of an earlier pidgin Portuguese with some Spanish influence. In Surinam, formerly Dutch Guiana, there are two creoles: Taki-Taki, which is spoken by city dwellers in Paramaribo; and Saramacca, which is spoken by the Bush Negroes, descendants of seventeenth-century slaves who escaped into the bush and intermarried with Indians. Saramacca developed from an English-based pidgin and contains numerous African survivals. Both Taki-Taki and Saramacca contain survivals of the Guianese pidgin Portuguese spoken in colonial times.[13]

While "Negro Dutch" was not a creole, the folk culture it transmitted was. For example, Prince collected the following example of Afro-Dutch folklore in the black dialect of Jersey Dutch, which his informant, the above-mentioned William De Freece, described as a cure for rheumatism.

Negro Charm

Altait an zomer
Stat de zuve bome;
Aske'n aike an al de lang vorbai

Kan nit rolle. Wat er opstat?

[Always in summer
Stand the seven trees;
Ash and oak and all along past
They cannot proceed. What are they standing on?]

De Freece told Prince that the seven trees symbolized seven stars. Prince described this charm as "incomprehensible" and suggested that the last line should read *kan nit rade wat er opstat,* meaning "I cannot guess what they are standing on."[14]

What Prince failed to realize, however, is that this charm is also a riddle. The answer to the riddle is that the trees are stars, which explains why they are standing on nothing. But there is something else at work here too. Art historian Robert Farris Thompson has shown that aspects of the traditional Kongo civilization, which encompassed present-day Zaire and the adjacent areas of Cabinda, Congo-Brazzaville, Gabon, and Angola, were brought to the Americas, especially to Cuba and Brazil. These included cosmological drawings, called cosmograms, which were used for initiation rituals and the mediation of spiritual power between the worlds of the living and the dead, and the supernatural uses of trees, staffs, branches, and roots. From the Brazilian priests of the folk religion known as Macumba, in Rio de Janeiro, Thompson collected a cosmogram that depicted "a Latin cross within a Star of David within a circle decorated with six minor stars."[15] Thus, this "Negro Charm" collected by Prince may well have been a survival of the cosmological belief system of the Bakongo people that ascribes a magical significance to the motif of seven stars.

There are numerous examples of the adoption of Dutch culture on the part of the Dutch-owned slaves. They used Dutch personal names, were married and baptised in the Dutch Reformed Church, and celebrated Dutch holidays. For example, in 1789 Alexander Coventry, a Scottish physician living in Hudson, New York, described in his diary how one slave observed the Dutch holiday of Paas (Easter).

> Saturday, 11 April . . . Van Curen's negro Cuff came to me in the morning. I asked if he would live with me. He said he would; he helped to drive the cows home to fodder, and when we got home, Van Curen was there at the house, and I agreed to purchase his negro at the price agreed upon yesterday. Cuff wanted to go over the creek to get some hoop poles which he had there, and he wanted two days next week to keep Paas.[16]

This passage shows an Africanism coexisting with the adoption of Dutch customs. The name of the slave, Cuff, is a shortened variant of Cuffee or Cuffy, the West African "day name" (personal name) associated with Friday. A male child born on Friday would be named Cuffee.[17] Yet the fact that Cuff wanted to celebrate Easter for two days is significant, because Paas was a two-day holiday in the Dutch tradition. It was the custom to bake special holiday cakes, known as Paas-cakes. According to Elizabeth L. Gebhard's 1909 memoir of life in Clover Reach, New York, "the making and baking of these cakes was a special feat of the slaves in most of the households. . . . There was a great rivalry among the colored people as to which could throw the Paas-cakes the highest and still successfully catch them."[18]

Pinkster is the Dutch name for Pentecost or Whitsunday, the feast that celebrates the appearance of the Holy Ghost to the disciples after Christ's crucifixion. Among the Dutch, their slaves, and the free blacks in New York and New Jersey, the commemoration took on the characteristics of a festival. On June 4, 1786, Coventry noted in his diary:

> It is all frolicing to-day with the Dutch and the Negro. This is a holy day, Whitsunday, called among the Dutch "Pinkster," and they have eggs boiled in all sorts of colors, and eggs cooked in every way, and everybody must eat all the eggs he can. And the frolicing is still kept up among the young folks, so that little else is done to-day but eat eggs and be jolly.[19]

There is evidence that grafted onto the Dutch celebration of Pinkster were African cultural survivals, suggesting that it was akin to the carnival celebrations in New Orleans, the Caribbean, and South America.

The central figure in the Pinkster celebration in Albany, circa 1800, was a slave known only as King Charles. He was memorialized in a poem written by an Absalom Aimwell (probably a nom de plume) titled *A Pinkster Ode for the Year 1803. Most Respectfully Dedicated to CAROLUS AFRICANUS REX: Thus Rendered in English: KING CHARLES, Captain-General and Commander in Chief of the PINKSTER BOYS*. While it is written from an ethnocentric, European point of view, the poem describes the celebration that took place on the day following Whitsunday on Pinkster Hill, the site of the present state capitol in Albany. It recounts how King Charles was "nobly born" and how he was brought to America as a slave, although still retaining "his native majesty." The poem describes how King Charles would lead the Guinea Dance, dressed in "his Pinkster clothes" with "his hat of yellow lace." Other observers than Aimwell noted that King Charles was a "Guinea man" from Angola, who lived to the ripe old age of 125. His costume was that of a British general. According to historian Joel Munsell, "he was nearly bare-legged, wore a red military coat trimmed profusely with variegated ribbons, and a small black hat with a pom-pom stuck on one side."

The reference to the Guinea Dance suggests an African survival. The dances, according to Munsell, were "the original Congo dances as danced in their [the dancers'] native Africa." He described it as a "double-shuffle, heel-and-toe breakdown." The poem mentions the musical instruments used to accompany the dance, including the fiddle, the banjo, the drum, the pipe, the tabor, the flute, the fife, and the jew's harp. James Eights's eyewitness account notes that the dance was called the Toto Dance; that the drums were "eel-pots covered with dressed sheepskin"; and that there was a song with an African refrain, "Hi-a-bomba-bomba-bomba."[20]

The so-called Guinea Dance might possibly have been a version of the Afro-Brazilian candomble, which is described as a "shuffle with small two-stepping foot twists in a counterclockwise circle," or perhaps it was similar to the Holy Dance or Shout of the Gullah blacks of the Carolina coast, which "proceeds in a heel-shuffle, with hand-clapping called 'patting the juba.'" The Toto Dance and the African refrain "Hi-a-bomba-bomba-bomba" are strikingly similar to descriptions of vodun dances, such as the Bamboula and the Calinda, performed between 1817 and 1885 in Congo Square in New Orleans. While some of the instruments mentioned in Aimwell's poem are European, the drums, banjo, and tabor are African. It is of note that the tradition of fife and drum corps performing blues riffs continues today among African Americans in the Mississippi Delta.[21]

Pinkster was also celebrated by blacks in New Jersey, in New York City, and on Long Island. While traveling through Dutch settlements along the Passaic River Valley of New Jersey in 1797, William Dunlap noted that "it is holiday they call pinkster and every public house is crowded with merry makers and waggon's full of rustic beaux and belles met us at every mile. The blacks as well as their masters were frolicking."[22] And in his 1845 romance *Satanstoe,* James Fenimore Cooper noted the African survivals in the Pinkster celebration on the commons in New York City (the site of present-day City Hall).

> By this time, nine tenths of the blacks of the city, and of the whole country within thirty or forty miles, indeed, were collected in thousands in those fields [the Pinkster ground], beating banjoes, singing African songs, drinking, and worst of all, laughing in a way that seemed to set their very hearts rattling within their ribs. . . . The features that distinguish a Pinkster frolic from the usual scenes at fairs, and other merry-makings, however, were of African origin. It is true, there are not now, nor were there then, many blacks of African birth; but the traditions and usages of their original country were so far preserved as to produce a marked difference between this festival, and one of European origin. Among other things, some were making music, by beating on skins drawn over the ends of hollow logs, while others were dancing to it, in a manner to show that they felt infinite delight. This, in particular, was said to be a usage of their African progenitors.[23]

Ironically, the celebration of Pinkster on Long Island survived longer among the Afro-Dutch than among the white Dutch. In 1874 local historian Gabriel Forman wrote: "Poor *Pinckster* has lost its rank among the festivals, and is only kept by the negroes; with them, especially on the west end of this island, it is still much of a holiday."[24]

Black studies professor A. J. Williams-Myers emphasizes the Africanisms in Pinkster, arguing that although the holiday had Dutch origins, "it was taken over by African slaves who incorporated into it their African traditions." Black nationalist historian Sterling Stuckey sees Pinkster as an example of a nation-wide African American culture that evolved after the Revolution. Historian Shane White, however, has taken issue with both. He maintains that "Pinkster was not simply an African survival transplanted to the New World, but a complex syncretization of African and Dutch cultures forged on the Hudson River within the context of American slavery." White argues that after the Revolutionary War, the Dutch underwent an "Americanization" process by which they abandoned many of their distinctive customs, at the same time that freed blacks from the countryside who migrated to the cities of Albany and New York revitalized Pinkster. He reaches this conclusion by noting that there are no written descriptions of Afro-Dutch Pinkster prior to the late eighteenth and early nineteenth centuries. Thus, both Stuckey and White see the Revolution as a watershed period. However, as others have noted, the Americanization of Dutch culture can be traced back to the Great Awakening, a quarter of a century earlier, and there was a significant African American presence in New York City throughout the eighteenth century.[25] Furthermore, a careful reading of the Pinkster sources indicates that it was not solely, or even primarily, an urban phenomenon. No matter when it originated, its distinctive Dutch components make it more appropriate to view Pinkster as an example of a regional Afro-Dutch culture than of a national African American culture.

Notwithstanding the African survivals in Afro-Dutch music and dance, there were also obvious European influences. Nowhere is this clearer than in the numerous historic references to Afro-Dutch musicians who played the fiddle, a European instrument. A 1741 advertisement for a runaway slave named Claus from New Brunswick, New Jersey, noted that "he is a Fiddler, and took his Fiddle with him. He uses the Bow with his left hand." In Bergen County, according to local historian John Hosey Osborn, "the different taverns in the country held dances to entertain the young people. . . . The music would be furnished by a fiddler, usually a slave from one of the farms, making some money after his day's work was done." There is a photograph in

Osborn's book, *Life in the Old Dutch Homesteads,* of two blacks in a barnyard, one holding a shotgun and the other a fiddle. It is captioned "Yon the fiddler and Sam the witchdoctor." A legend was told among blacks in Brooklyn about how a black servant "beat the Devil" in a fiddle competition at Martense's Lane. As recently as 1967, ethnomusicologist Charles H. Kaufman collected fiddle tunes from Jimmy De Freese, one of the Ramapo Mountain People living in Ringwood, New Jersey. The tunes included many from the British Isles, such as "The Fisher's Hornpipe," "The Irish Washerwoman," and "Buck and Wing" (also known as "The Turkey in the Straw").[26]

One intriguing example of Afro-Dutch folklore is the fragment of a slave song collected in Bergen County in the nineteenth century. It appeared in an 1888 issue of *The Landscape,* an amateur newspaper published by Alfred P. Smith, a black resident of Saddle River, New Jersey.

> A bit of song of the "good old times" in New Jersey has
> come down to us from the following lines, which used to
> be sung by the slaves in Bergen County:
>
>> Cold, frosty morning
>> Nigger berry good.
>> Wid his axe on his shoulder,
>> And way to the wood.
>> Wid a piece of cold pancake,
>> And a little hog's fat,
>> And de grumble like the debble,
>> If you get too much of dat.[27]

This folk song is of interest for several reasons. First and foremost, it is a protest by the slaves against the harsh conditions of their servitude. Secondly, it is secular. Historian Lawrence Levine has argued that the worldview of black slaves, like that of their African ancestors, was essentially a sacred one. The secular worldview did not develop until after emanicipation. Levine argues that under slavery secular songs were secondary to spirituals, and that after the Civil War, secular songs, such as the blues, became increasingly important. However, as folklorist Robert B. Winans has noted, Levine overlooked a large body of secular slave songs, such as those transcribed in the WPA slave narratives.[28]

Not every component of Afro-Dutch culture can be traced back to Dutch or African originals. In 1955 K. Leroy Irvis, who was born in Saugerties, New York, with Afro-Dutch ancestry on both sides of his family, wrote an article titled "Negro Tales from Eastern New York" for the *New York Folklore Quarterly*. In it he wrote:

> We are York State folks. For as long as anyone in my mother's family can remember, the men of the family wandered the West Shore valley of the Hudson from Kingston to Albany. They were Ten Broecks, Cantines, and Van Ettens; they were Dutch and proud of it. I can remember my Aunt Serbania telling me about her great-grandmother, a stern old lady who both spoke and understood English, but who refused to speak it except in the privacy of her home. In public she spoke Dutch, as any proper person should. . . . My father's family has an equally long history in the state, but on the other side of the river. . . . They were all "East-shorers" . . . were, that is, until my father crossed the river and then went north to Albany with my mother.[29]

Irvis noted that the tales he had been told since childhood were not black folktales; they were just folktales. But this is not quite accurate. His tale about the old witch of Glasco, Ulster County, is about a black woman. Several of his stories deal with race relations between blacks and whites, including one trickster tale in which a black outsmarts a white. Many of the tales Mr. Irvis remembered from his childhood were, by his own account, similar to tales told him by a southern black from Virginia. In other words, these were a feature, but not the distinguishing feature, of Afro-Dutch culture.

Finally, the nature of Afro-Dutch folklife may be embodied in an ambiguous piece of folk art: a cigar store figure of an Indian princess, now housed in the museum of the New York State Historical Association in Cooperstown. The museum acquired it from Jean Lipman, the folk art collector and writer, who noted that oral tradition attributed it to a black named Job from Freehold, New Jersey. A search of nineteenth century census records for Monmouth County does not confirm this information. Nevertheless, the carved wooden figure does show distinct African influences in the masklike face, the long tubular arms, and the sensuous breasts. Yet this is not an African sculpture. It lacks the religious dimension characteristic of African art. Rather, it is a European trade sign. Thus, like Afro-Dutch culture itself, it is African, European, and African American. At the same time it is none of these, but rather a unique, regional American product.

3

THE ORIGIN OF
THE "PINEYS"

Despite its great size—about one million acres, or one-fifth of the the state's land area—there has always been something elusive about the New Jersey Pine Barrens. Named for its dominant tree species, the pitch pine (*Pinus rigida*), the region is a mosaic of swamps, bogs, marshes, and forests of oak, cedar, and pine. Below its sandy, porous soil is the Cohansey aquifer, an underground reservoir of fresh water. The region has been called a "barrens," because it initially impressed Europeans as not suitable for farming. Today some people prefer the term Pinelands, or simply "the Pines."

Even the geographic extent of the region is vague, in part because zones of vegetation, soil, and culture do not have exact boundaries. The Pinelands have been delimited differently at different times. In 1916 botanist John W. Harshberger mapped the region according to vegetation. On the east he drew the boundary line just west of Barnegat Bay, on the southwest well north of Delaware Bay, and on the north well into Monmouth County. The Pinelands National Reserve, created by the United States Congress in 1978, differs significantly from Harshberger's Pine Barrens and includes parts of Barnegat Bay and Long Beach Island, the barrier island east of Barnegat Bay. On the south it reaches to the shore of Delaware Bay, but only as far west as the Maurice River, while on the northeast it excludes the southern part of Monmouth County included by Harshberger. Harshberger's map followed natural boundaries, while the map of the Pinelands National Reserve uses highways as boundaries in some places.[1]

On the other hand, when folklorist Herbert Halpert collected folk tales and folk songs in the Pines between 1936 and 1941, he confined his fieldwork to Ocean County and the eastern part of Burlington County. His rationale was that the region north of the Mullica River was not suited for agriculture and therefore was the true Pine Barrens.[2] However, when the American Folklife Center of the Library of Congress conducted the Pinelands Folklife Project in the fall of 1983, they accepted the boundaries established by the Pinelands National Reserve. We need not say that one set of boundaries is right and the other wrong; the point is that the region has been defined in a variety of ways.

As elusive as the region are the people known as the "Pineys." Janice Sherwood of Forked River, one of the founding members of the Pinelands Culture Society, says: "We just figure if you gotta ask what a Piney is, then you haven't been there long enough to figure it out. But I think a Piney is just a little bit deeper in the woods than you are." Social distinctions are implied in the current folk terminology: the "Pineys" are those who live in the interior, the "Clam Diggers" are the baymen along the coast, and the "Rock Jumpers" are the farmers south of the Mullica River.[3] In the late 1930s and early 1940s, when Herbert Halpert asked who the Pineys were, he was repeatedly told that the Pineys lived further south—until he reached a point in his travels when he was told that the Pineys lived further north. At that time no one admitted to being a Piney. Today people from all over southern New Jersey proudly proclaim themselves Pineys, some even sporting "Piney Power" bumper stickers and buttons.

The name has had a shifting referent. Some families that have lived only one or two generations in southern New Jersey have adopted a "Piney" identity. Joe and George Albert are a case in point. Two brothers from Sayreville in north central New Jersey, they frequently visited the region on hunting and fishing expeditions. In 1939 Joe Albert moved to Waretown to live in a cabin he had built there, and in the late 1950s his brother George retired and moved in with him. Their cabin, known as the "Old Home Place," became the site of a weekly musical gathering, the "Saturday Night Jamboree." From this informal gathering evolved in 1975 the Pinelands Cultural Society, which holds weekly performances featuring local musicians, including a string band known as the Pineconers. Gladys Eayre of the Pineconers is a descendant of an old southern New Jersey family. But the Pineconers' banjo player, Sam Hunt, although he was Joe and George Albert's hunting guide, was not born in the Pine Barrens; he moved to the Barnegat Bay vicinity as a boy.[4]

The connotation of the name "Piney" also has changed. Throughout the nineteenth century and well into the twentieth, the name had a negative connotation. It was in use as early as 1866, when G. T. Le Boutillier, a student at Princeton who was sent as a missionary to the village of Shamong, wrote to Rev. Allen H. Brown of the Presbyterian Church in Mays Landing:

> The people who inhabit this region are the original, who have long resided here and new comers who are rapidly establishing towns and villages here and there throughout it. The former, commonly called "Pinies," are a sparse

population living and obtaining a livelihood by making
charcoal, gathering cranberries and huckleberries for the
markets. They are sadly ignorant, and superstitious, and
degraded.[5]

A few years earlier, in 1859, W. F. Mayer, writing in the *Atlantic
Monthly,* used the term "Pine Rats" to refer to the people residing in the
Pine Barrens and described them in the most derogatory terms.

Completely besotted and brutish in their ignorance, they
are incapable of obtaining an honest living, and have supported themselves, from a time which may be called imme-
morial, by practising petty larceny on an organized plan.
The Pine rat steals wood, steals game, steals cranberries,
steals anything, in fact, that his hand can be laid upon; and
woe to the property of the man who dares attempt to
restrain him.

The residents of the southern New Jersey interior did not fit neatly
into Mayer's Jeffersonian vision of idyllic farmsteads, and so he advo-
cated their removal from the landscape.

We shall not suffer his company much longer in this
world,—poor, neglected, pitiable, darkened soul that he
is, this fellow-citizen of ours. He must move on; for civilization, like a stern, prosaic policeman, will have no idlers
in the past. There must be no vagrants, not even in the forest. . . . We must have farms here, and happy homesteads,
and orchards, . . . instead of silent aisles and avenues of
mournful pine-trees, sheltering such forlorn miscreations
as our poor cranberry-stealing friends! . . . There is no
room for a gypsy in all our wide America! The [Pine] Rat
must follow the Indian,—must fade like breath from a
windowpane in winter![6]

Not all comments on the dwellers in the Pines were as offensive as this one. An 1891 article about "Jersey lightning" (applejack) in a Burlington County newspaper gives them the name "pine-hawkers."

> In Southampton, where applejack is plenty and pine-hawkers numerous, it is invariably prescribed for chills and fever, grippe, coughs, colds and nervous prostration. Owley Lemon, king of the pine-hawkers, who is now 76 years of age, has been drinking applejack regularly ever since the Civil War broke out, and even now can drink a quart per day without the slightest inconvenience. . . . Despite his years, he can kick higher, dance longer and stand more exposure than any man in Southampton.

In an 1893 article on "Jerseyisms" in *Dialect Notes,* Francis B. Lee included the term "piners," which he defined as "those who live in the Jersey pines—the 'ridge' sections (eastern and southern) of the state." According to an 1894 article in *Harper's New Monthly Magazine,* "the term 'piners' is synonymous with the term 'poor whites' in the South."[7]

Elizabeth S. Kite, a staff member of the Vineland Training School, made reference both to "Pineys" and "Pine Rats" in an article she wrote in 1913: "They are known as the 'Pineys' or 'Pine Rats' and are recognized as a distinct people by the normal communities living on the borders of their forests, although their manner of living arouses neither surprise nor interest, having always been taken quite as a matter of course."

Miss Kite performed the fieldwork for the 1913 study of "the heredity of feeblemindedness" in the Kallikak family. This study was conducted by the Vineland Training School under the direction of Henry H. Goddard and followed the approach first used in the 1870s in the famous study of the genetics of criminology in the Jukes family of upstate New York. It was generally assumed that the "Kallikaks" (a pseudonym used to protect the identity of the family being studied) were residents of the New Jersey Pine Barrens, but psychologist J. David Smith has proven conclusively that the Kallikak family lived in Hunterdon County, well to the north.[8]

The association of the Kallikak study with the Pineys may have stemmed from the fact that Miss Kite wrote an article about the Pineys using a similar approach. In it she reinforced the stereotype of the Pineys as shiftless and degenerate.

> The real Piney has no inclination to labor, submitting to every privation in order to avoid it. Lazy, lustful and cunning, he is a degenerate creature who has learned to provide for himself the bare necessities of life without entering into life's stimulating struggle. Like the degenerate relative of the crab that ages ago gave up a free roving life and, gluing its head to a rock, built a wall of defense around itself, spending the rest of its life kicking food into its mouth and enjoying the functionings of reproduction, the Piney and all the rest of his type have become barnacles upon our civilization, all the higher functions of whose manhood have been atrophied through disuse.

In later years Miss Kite attempted to modify the harshness of her stereotype of the Pineys. In 1940 she told folklorist Herbert Halpert, "Nothing would give me greater pleasure than to correct the idea that has unfortunately been given by the newspapers regarding the Pines. Anybody who has lived in the Pines was a Piney. I think it a most terrible calamity that the newspaper publicity took the term and gave it the degenerate sting."[9] Halpert did not confront Miss Kite with the words she had written twenty-seven years earlier.

Associated with the term "Pineys" is a legend about their origins. The development of this legend can be traced through written sources. In fact, there is no evidence that the legend either originated in or became part of oral tradition. Created and sustained by local historians and popular writers, it should be considered a local-history legend. I distinguish between a local-history legend and a folk legend. A local-history legend is a narrative set in the past that is loosely or not at all tied to historical documentation and that is elaborated upon by local historians in a chain of written communication. A folk legend, on the other hand, is transmitted by a chain of oral communication.

The earliest mention of this local-history legend is in the 1859 article in the *Atlantic Monthly* mentioned above. The account asserts that the Pineys were descendants of Revolutionary War Tories who sought refuge in the Pine Barrens.

> This extraordinary race of beings are lineal descendants of the New Jersey Tories, who, during the Revolution, made the Pines their refuge, whence they sallied in perpetual forays against the farms and dwellings of the partisans of the opposite cause. Several hundred of these fanatical desperadoes made the forest their home, and laid waste the surrounding townships by their sudden raids.[10]

An 1894 article in *Harper's New Monthly Magazine* distinguished between the "Tory Refugees" and the so-called "Pine Robbers," who conducted raids on the surrounding farms from their base in the Pines: "The Jersey Pines were first brought to the notice of the great world beyond them as a place of hiding of many Tory refugees during the war for our independence. These were British loyalists who helped to give Monmouth County the character it earned as the chief sufferer, in that bloody contention, of the horrors that always attend civil war." The author noted that some of the Refugees were New Jersey militia-

men who became Loyalists; others were renegades who were nominally Loyalists, paid by Tories in New York to hide in the woods and
plunder the countryside; and still others were marauders who escaped
from British vessels to form "picarooning" bands. The Refugees were
known as the "Jersey Greens" as distinct from the New Jersey soldiers
in the Continental Army, who were called the "Jersey Blues."

> These precious opponents of liberty did not pause at trifles
> like murdering sleeping men, but they were charming
> when compared with the Pine robbers. So desperately bad
> were these robbers that they preyed upon both sides, and
> the names and deeds of their leader are kept in mind today
> through the legends of old neighborhoods and the tradi-
> tions of old families.[11]

By the time of Elizabeth Kite's 1913 article, the legend had
grown to include not only Tories and Pine Robbers, but also (in the
words of Kite's subtitle) " 'Disowned' Friends, . . . Hessians, Revellers
from Joseph Bonaparte's Court at Bordentown, and other Sowers of
Wild Oats." According to Kite, "in the Province of New Jersey, it is
certain that 'disowned' youth, cast out by the society [of Friends] did
in some cases betake themselves to the loose lives of the dwellers of the
Pines." In addition, she stated, "after the battle of Trenton, certain
Hessian soldiers and other deserters from the British army found
safety in the seclusion of the Pines, and added still another element to
this already mixed population." In reference to the followers of Joseph
Bonaparte, Kite wrote:

> In the gay days when Prince Joseph Bonaparte held his
> miniature court at Bordentown, many were the revels and
> hunting parties in the Pines, which were indulged in by
> the members of his suite. All these revelers came back,
> leaving a train of nameless offspring to complicate still

further the mixed social problem of the Pines, so that today, in tracing the ancestry of any particular group, one runs up continually against the impossibility of proving exact ancestry.[12]

In 1936 local historian Henry Charlton Beck defined the Pineys as those "who lonely in lack of education, have lived back in the Jersey pine woods, on hidden trails and beside dismal swamps." He wrote that they are "the descendants of first settlers, bog ore miners, lumber-cutters, glassmakers, sailors and soldiers of Washington's time, Hessians who preferred to go amuck in the woods to returning home, [and] slaves who sought strange ways to celebrate their new-found liberty." Evidently, he was influenced by the stereotype of the Pineys fostered by Elizabeth Kite and others when he referred to the Pineys as "the children and grandchildren of those to whom several wives for one man was an accepted code." He recounted one legend in particular.

One story, perhaps the most persistent in this regard, is well known. A British soldier of good parentage but with uncertain ideas of living, became enamored of a barmaid in a wayside tavern and without the trouble of a wedding they became joint proprietors of the place. There came a family of eight children, all of whom were later found to have mental deficiencies or criminal inclinations. The soldier, tiring of this mode of life, went back to England, married in his rightful class and began anew. At home a family of three normal children resulted.[13]

This story is suspiciously similar to the genealogy of the Kallikak family, which, according to Henry H. Goddard, descended from a soldier whom Goddard gave the pseudonym Martin Kallikak, Sr.

When Martin Sr., of the good family, was a boy of fifteen, his father died, leaving him without parental care or oversight. Just before attaining his majority, the young man joined one of the numerous military companies that were formed to protect the country at the beginning of the Revolution. At one of the taverns frequented by the militia he met a feeble-minded girl by whom he became the father of a feeble-minded son. This child was given, by its mother, the name of the father in full, and thus has been handed down to posterity the father's name and the mother's mental capacity.[14]

While the soldier in the Kallikak study was on the American side rather than the British, the similarity of the two stories suggests that Beck had picked up a version of the Kallikak legend and applied it to the Pineys.

Perhaps the most widely read version of the legend about the origins of the Pineys is found in John McPhee's 1967 book *The Pine Barrens,* which originally appeared in the *New Yorker.* He speaks of the Tories who fled to the Pines during the American Revolution. "People with names like Britton and Brower, loyal to the King, and sometimes covered with feather and tar, left their homes in Colonial cities and took refuge in the Pine Barrens." He also mentions the Hessians. "After the British defeats at Trenton and Princeton, Hessian soldiers deserted the British Army in considerable numbers, and some of them went into the Pine Barrens." He claims, for example, that "Sooy is a German name more common in the pines than Smith." McPhee also repeats the part of the legend about the Quakers: "Also during the eighteenth century, when the farmlands of western New Jersey were heavily populated with Quakers, the Pine Barrens served as a catch basin for Quakers who could not live up to the standards of the Quaker code." He cites the Ridgway family as an example. In addition, McPhee mentions English, Welsh, and Scots who came primarily by way of

New England, including the Cranmer family, said to be descended from Thomas Cranmer, the archbishop of Canterbury; and French Huguenots who settled at Mt. Misery, including the Bozarth family. Some blacks "fled from slavery into the pines," including Dr. James Still, the so-called "Doctor of the Pines." There were also descendants of Lenape Indians from the Brotherton Reservation. "Numerous people in the Pine Barrens today are descended, in part, from Indians who remained. George Crummel, a charcoal-maker who lived in Jenkins Neck, and who died there in 1964, was the great-grandson of Isaac Cromo, a chief of the Leni [sic] Lenape." Finally, McPhee rounds out the picture with pirates, privateers, smugglers, and Pine Robbers, including Joseph Mulliner, who led a band of outlaws and "became a legend in the pines."[15]

Some folklorists think that the factuality of a legend is irrelevant; what matters is not what happened in the past but what people think happened. Legends tell us much about the values of the people who believe and transmit them. Contrary to popular misconception, not all legends are devoid of historical fact. Some are historically verifiable; some are contradicted by the historical evidence; and some are compounded of historical fact and creative imagination.[16] By examining the relationship between the historical record and these legendary accounts of the past one gains insights into how the legends were created and how they function in the lives of those who believe them. To this end, the various components in the legend of "Piney" origins must be individually evaluated.

The idea that the Pineys are descended in part from Indians on the Brotherton Reservation is unlikely. The Brotherton Reservation was established at what is today Indian Mills in Burlington County in 1758, during the French and Indian War. The Indians who resided at Brotherton were primarily from central New Jersey. By the mid-eighteenth century they were concentrated in two locations: at Bethel or Cranbury in Middlesex County and at Crosswicks in Mercer County. Their number was relatively small. In 1746 David Brainerd, a Presbyterian missionary to the Indians at Crosswicks, estimated that there were about 250 Lenape Indians there. In 1759 Governor Francis Bernard wrote that the number of Indians at Brotherton "does not amount to 200 & when We have gathered together all in the province they will not be 300." The implication is that not all the Lenape in New Jersey lived on the reservation. There was, for example, a small group residing "off reservation" at Weepink, about ten miles from Brotherton, near present-day Vincentown. Moreover, the population of Brotherton declined rapidly. In 1774, according to Governor William Franklin, only about fifty to sixty Indians resided there. In 1802, when the reservation was disbanded, a report to the governor mentioned that sixty-three adults had rights to the land. In the same year, it is reported that seventy to eighty Lenape moved from Brotherton to New Stockbridge, New York. It is not known how many, if any, Lenape may have remained in New Jersey; however, there is little or no evidence that they contributed significantly to the ancestry of the Pineys.[17]

By the time of the Brotherton Reservation, many of the Lenape had adopted European surnames. We know the names of at least those Indians who attended various treaty conferences and signed the treaties. Many of the same names appear on land deeds of the same period.[18] Thus, we know the names of many of the last Lenape in New Jersey, and they are not the same as those of the various individuals and groups claiming Indian ancestry who began to appear on the fringes of the Pine Barrens in the nineteenth century. Most of the latter were listed in the manuscript censuses as "black" or "mulatto." Their descendants claim that the census listed Indians, especially those who had a racially mixed ancestry, as "blacks." In fact, for much of the nineteenth century the United States census did not include Indians at all.

One of these supposed Lenape descendants was George Crummel, called by John McPhee "the Indian Collier of Jenkins Neck." According to local historians Robert J. Sim and Harry B. Weiss, George H. Crummel was born near Sykesville. His father, George Henry Crummel, came from the vicinity of Hornerstown and died about 1915. The 1880 census lists a George H. Cromwell (not Crummel), age twelve, residing with his parents Charles and Phoebe Cromwell in the township of Eatontown, Monmouth County. Their race was listed as "black." It is probable that this was the father of the George Crummel mentioned by McPhee; and if this is true, his grandfather was not an Indian named Isaac Cromo, as McPhee states, but a black named Charles Cromwell. The name Isaac Cromo does not appear on any deeds or treaties. Furthermore, the 1830 census lists no Crummels, but it includes Cromwells as "free Negro heads of families" in Burlington and Monmouth Counties. A black named Oliver Cromwell of Burlington County served as a private in the New Jersey Continental Line from 1777 to 1781 and he fought at the battles of Trenton, Brandywine, Princeton, Monmouth, and Yorktown.[19] Finally, the surname Cromwell is not one of those associated with the known Lenape.

Perhaps the only person who could claim a genealogical link with the Lenape was a woman known as "Indian Ann." She was a familiar figure in Vincentown and Medford around the turn of the century. She supported herself by making baskets and picking cranberries and blueberries. One account states that she was the daughter of a Rancocas Indian named Ash Tamar. Another source indicates that her father was Chief Elisha Moses Ashatama, who lived in Egg Harbor at the time of the War of 1812, and that she married twice. Her first husband was Peter Green; her second, John Roberts, a black. Her will, dated 1884, mentions three sons, three daughters, and a house with land in Shamong Township. The agreement by which the Indians at Brotherton ceded the rights to their land was signed by, among others, an Indian named Ashatoma. Thus, Indian Ann at least was linked by genealogical association with a known Indian at the Brotherton Reservation. Ann Roberts appears in the 1880 manuscript census as an "Indian," living in Shamong; she was one of the only people in New Jersey so listed in the nineteenth-century census. But her birthplace was given as New York, which was also the place of birth listed for her mother and father.[20] If the census was accurate, she probably was not the daughter of Ashatoma, nor, for that matter, a Lenape Indian. All we can say for certain is that she lived near the site of the Brotherton Reservation and followed an occupation that had been traditional among the Lenape in the eighteenth century.

There were other self-designated Indians whose claims are even harder to assess. James Still, the "Doctor of the Pines," mentions in his autobiography that there was an Indian family named Moore that lived nearby when he was growing up in Shamong Township. "Our nearest neighbors were an Indian family, the name of whose head was Job Moore. His eldest son was named Job, and he and I were very social. We played together and fished and hunted when the opportunity would admit." Still notes: "I was also afraid of Indian Job. He was a tall man, I think six feet and six inches high. He would often get drunk, and go whooping about in Indian fashion, which was a great terror to me."[21] However, we have no other record of "Indian Job" and his family.

In addition to individuals, there were two groups living on the fringes of the Pine Barrens that claimed Indian ancestry. One group resided in Monmouth County, in two locations: at Reevytown in what is today Tinton Falls and at Sand Hill in present-day Neptune. Those in Neptune called themselves the "Sand Hill Indians." The surnames associated with this group include Reevy, Richardson, and Crummel. The names Reevy, Richardson, and Cromwell (which may be a variant of Crummel) appear in the 1830 census not as Indians, but as "free

Negro heads of families." In the 1950s, the "Sand Hill Indians" disbanded, but one of their descendants runs the New Jersey Indian Office, a private organization in Orange, New Jersey.

The other group claiming Indian ancestry resides in the Gouldtown settlement near Bridgeton, in Cumberland County. The surnames there include Gould, Pierce, and Murray—families that also were listed in the 1830 census as black. Some of them have intermarried with the Nanticoke Indians, a racially mixed group in Delaware, and have consequently introduced the surnames Harmon and Ridgeway into the community.[22]

We have already cited the interesting legend of Gouldtown's origins, according to which the community descends from an illicit union between the granddaughter of John Fenwick, one of the proprietors of West New Jersey, and a black man named Gould (see chapter 1).[23] The striking similarity between the Gouldtown and Kallikak legends leads one to speculate that perhaps the story of John Fenwick's granddaughter was the inspiration for the Kallikak account.

The idea that renegade Quakers contributed to the "Piney" population is essentially true. Many of the surnames of the people in the Pine Barrens are Quaker names found throughout southern New Jersey. Take, for example, the Ridgways, the Cranmers, and the Ongs. Local residents take pains to note that Ridgway is spelled without an *e*, perhaps to distinguish themselves from the Nanticoke Ridgeways (mentioned above). The first Ridgway in the region was a Quaker named Richard Ridgway, who with his wife Elizabeth, came from Welford, England to Bucks County, Pennsylvania in 1677. He resided in Pennsylvania until about 1690, when he moved to Burlington County, New Jersey, where he served as a judge from 1700 to 1720. He died in 1723. Some time prior to 1714, Thomas Ridgway of upper Burlington County, probably a relative of Richard, settled in Little Egg Harbor. He was listed as a member of the Friends Meeting in Tuckerton. The Cranmer family descends from William Cranmer, an early settler at Southold, Long Island, not Thomas Cranmer, the archbishop of Canterbury, as stated by McPhee. William Cranmer moved to Forked River and then to Cedar Creek, New Jersey, in the late 1740s and was also listed as a member of the Friends Meeting at Tuckerton. Ong is a famous Pinelands surname, because of Ong's Hat, a place name immortalized in a legend retold by local historian Henry Charlton Beck. Like Thomas Ridgway, Jacob Ong came from upper Burlington County and settled in Little Egg Harbor. He and his wife Elizabeth were elders in the Friends Meeting at Egg Harbor. In 1725 he left Egg Harbor to settle in Pennsylvania. He returned in 1728 and left again for Pennsylvania in 1735, this time never to return. Ong's Hat was probably named for Jacob Ong, even though the Ong family did not remain in the Pines. This information supports Pauline Miller's contention that many of the Piney families are branches of Quaker families that settled along the coast. The fact that many of the descendants of these Quakers became Methodists, which was the predominant religious denomination of the Pines after the Second Great Awakening, lends support to the tradition that "disaffected" Quakers supplied one strain of the Piney genealogy.[24]

On the other hand, the legendary contribution of the Hessian soldiers has no basis in historical fact—despite a cycle of tales collected by Herbert Halpert about Jerry Munyhun, "the wizard of the Pines," who was said to be a trickster and magician. One of Halpert's informants, Charles Grant, called Munyhun an "old Hanover Hessian," because stories about him were associated with the Hanover iron furnace in the Pines. Others, however, said that Munyhun was either Irish or black, and there is in fact no evidence that he ever existed.[25]

Furthermore, no Pinelands surnames appear on the lists of Hessian soldiers who fought in the American Revolution, and those Pinelands families thought to be Hessian do not have German names. For example, the Clevenger family, said to be Hessian by one local historian, has been traced to England. The first Clevenger in America was a George Clevenger, who resided in Yonkers, New York, some time before 1682. His son, John Clevenger, was born in 1678 and moved to Monmouth County, New Jersey, in 1699; records show that by 1757 he was living in New Hanover Township, Burlington County. The Sooy family, said to be German by John McPhee, was in fact Dutch. Their ancestor, Joost Sooy, was born in Holland in 1685 and immigrated to America about 1705. He was a mariner-merchant and appears in the records of the Old Dutch Reformed Church in New York. He and his family migrated to Cheesequake Creek in Monmouth County and then to Lower Bank on the Mullica River in Burlington County, and together with his sons he purchased thousands of acres in Washington Township. He died in 1767 and was buried at Lower Bank. The Bozarth family was German, not French Huguenot, as McPhee stated, but they are not descended from Hessian soldiers. Simon Bozoth of Evesham bought land in Burlington as early as 1715, well before the Revolutionary War. He died in Burlington County in 1753, according to family records. The family name (variously spelled Bosserdt, Boshart, and Bussart) is common among the Pennsylvania Dutch, who are themselves of German origin.[26]

It is of note that the legend about the origin of the Ramapo Mountain People also asserts Hessian ancestry (see chapter 1). Evidently, these German mercenaries who fought on the British side during the American Revolution have had a special appeal to local historians, who have seen them as the skeletons in the closets of more than one isolated group.

The idea that the Pineys descend from pirates is a mixture of some historical fact, some misunderstanding, and a lot of romantic elaboration. It is true that some pirates operated off the coast of New

Jersey in the early eighteenth century. According to colonial news-papers, in 1717 a pirate sloop commanded by a captain named Paul Williams raided two sloops and a brigantine off Sandy Hook, and in 1722 a pirate brigantine and a pirate sloop cruised in and out of Delaware Bay over a period of three weeks. However, legends about treasure buried by either Captain Kidd or Blackbeard have no basis in historical fact, although both William Kidd and William Teach (alias Blackbeard) were real people. Captain Kidd lived in New York City; in 1701 he was tried for piracy in England, convicted, and hanged. But, as historian J. Franklin Jameson noted, the difference between piracy and privateering was not always clear. By law a privateer was a pri-vately owned, armed vessel granted a letter of marque authorizing it to commit acts of warfare against an enemy. William Kidd had such a letter of marque from Lord Bellomont, the governor of New York. However, Captain Kidd's privateering/piracy activities were confined to the coast of Africa, during the height of the Madagascar slave trade and King William's War. William Teach's activities, on the other hand, were confined primarily to the Caribbean and the coast of North Carolina. There is no historical evidence that either man ever came to New Jersey, let alone buried treasure here.[27]

Nevertheless, legends persist about treasure buried by either Captain Kidd or Blackbeard along the Jersey Shore and the Delaware River. Usually, the buried treasure was protected by the ghost of a crewman, who had been killed for this purpose and buried with the treasure.

Though we can discount these romantic tales of buried treasure, there certainly was smuggling and privateering along the New Jersey coast. According to local historian Arthur Pierce, New Jersey had only three legal ports of entry during the 1760s: Perth Amboy, Cohansey, and Burlington. The Mullica River basin, especially in the vicinity of Little Egg Harbor, became the center for smuggling. Charles Read, collector of customs at Burlington, wrote in 1763 that "many vessels trading to Plantations not belonging to the King of Great Britain, returning with cargoes of Rum, Sugar, Molasses, have found means to smuggle the same into his Majesty's Plantations, without paying the King's Duty."[28] This smuggling should be viewed in the context of the British Navigation Laws, which were circumvented by some of the most respectable citizens in the American colonies, including John Hancock. Smuggling in New Jersey was also an assertion of economic independence from the dominance of the ports of New York and Philadelphia.

With the outbreak of the American Revolution, many of those who had been smugglers became privateers, including Joseph Sooy of Little Egg Harbor. Privateering was such a problem for the British that in September 1778 they dispatched from New York an expedition of three hundred British regulars and about one hundred New Jersey Loyalists under Captain Patrick Ferguson to "clean out the nest of Rebel pirates" at Chestnut Neck and then to proceed up the Mullica River to destroy the iron works at Batsto and the military storehouses at The Forks. Governor William Livingston of New Jersey dispatched Count Casimir Pulaski to intercept the British, but Pulaski got lost and ended up in Tuckerton. Three privateers and an armed pilot boat managed to escape before the British arrived at Chestnut Neck. The British destroyed the village, which Captain Ferguson described as "the principal resort of this nest of Pirates."[29] What the British called piracy the Americans considered patriotism. It was possibly this confusion between piracy and privateering that led local historians to give credit to stories of pirates and buried treasure in southern New Jersey.

The tradition that Tories, Pine Robbers, and Refugees lived in the Pines has some basis in historical fact. According to historian David J. Fowler, New Jersey had a disproportionate number of Tories, resulting in much civil violence along the coast and in the Pine

Barrens. Much of this activity occurred after the British surrender at Yorktown in 1781 and before the signing of the treaty that ended the Revolutionary War in 1783. Some Loyalists fought in organized units, such as the New Jersey Volunteers. Others, known as "Refugees," formed less formal bands, sometimes numbering as many as one hundred. Monmouth County was a center of Refugee activity, both in the Pine Barrens and at Sandy Hook. In 1782 Captain Joshua Huddy was hanged by a band of Refugees. There were also the so-called Pine Robbers, or "Pine Banditti," who seemed to be taking advantage of the unstable situation to raid both the Tory and Whig sides. The distinction between the Refugees and the Pine Robbers was not so clearly drawn.[30] Two Pine Robbers are of special interest to the legend of Piney origins: William Giberson and Joseph Mulliner.

Giberson was an old Pine Barrens name. Herbert Halpert collected a cycle of stories about Sam "the Fiddler" Giberson (1808–1884). The Giberson family was in fact Dutch, the name being originally Gysbertse. In 1634 Lubbert Gijberts, a wheelwright from Blaricum in the province of North Holland, came to Rensselaerswyck. In 1701 a John Gysbertse of Middletown was mentioned in a land deed. The family had ties to the village of Flatbush on Long Island, and by the time of the Revolution there were Gibersons living also in Ocean County. But while the Giberson family is found throughout South Jersey, there is no evidence that any of them are direct descendants of William Giberson, the Pine Robber.[31]

Legends about William Giberson date back to the mid-nineteenth century. In 1845 local historian Isaac Mickle wrote that a septuagenarian informant described Giberson as "a large man of almost incredible strength and activity," who "at a running jump . . . could clear the top of an ordinary Egg Harbor wagon." Mickle provided an account of how in December 1782 William Giberson was captured by some militiamen commanded by Captain John Davis. They had been sent to Egg Harbor to stop the Refugee activity there.

> On one occasion his lieutenant, Benjamin Bates, with Richard Powell, a private, called at a house where Davis had been informed, over night, that two Refugee officers were lodging. Bates got to the house before any of the family had risen except two girls who were making a fire in the kitchen.
>
> He inquired if there were any persons in the house besides the family, and was answered, "None, except two men from up in the country." He bade the girls to show him where they were, which they did. In passing through the room separating the kitchen from the bedroom, he saw the pistols lying on the table. Knocking at the door, he was at first refused admittance, but finding him determined to enter, the two Refugees finally let him in. They refused to tell their names but were afterwards found to be William Giberson and Henry Lane, Refugee lieutenants, the former a notorious rascal who had committed many outrages, and killed one or two Americans in cold blood. On their way to the quarters of Davis' company, Giberson called Bates' attention to something he pretended to see at a distance. Giberson started in another direction, and being a very fast runner, although Bates fired his musket at him, made his escape. Davis, on being informed of what happened, told Bates to try again the next night. Accordingly, the next night he went to the same house. While in the act of opening the door he heard the click of a musket cock, behind a large tree within a few feet of him, and turning

around, saw Giberson just taking aim at him. He dropped
on his knees and the ball cut the rim of his hat. Giberson
started to run, but before he had gone many rods Bates
gave him a load of buckshot which broke his leg. He was
well guarded until he could be removed with Lane to
Burlington gaol.[32]

According to David Fowler, this incident is confirmed by the pension
application filed in 1831 by Benjamin Bates. It recounts essentially the
same incident, but adds how Giberson later escaped from the Burlington County jail dressed in his sister's clothing. "He was afterward
taken to the Burlington County Gael, where he affected his Escape; his
sister having been permitted to visit him, they exchanged clothes. He
went out and she remained in prison and the plot was not discovered
until he had got too far to be overtaken."[33] This is normally the stuff of
which legends are made, yet for some reason this postscript did not
become part of the Giberson local-history legend.

In the 1920s local historian Alfred M. Heston recounted the
capture of William Giberson in *South Jersey: A History* (1924) and *New
Jersey Waggon Jaunts* (1926). He added another incident to the stories
about Giberson, which changed him from a worthless rogue into a
violent outlaw with a soft side.

It is related that one day a lad was gunning in Tuckerton
Bay, when he was surprised by the appearance of Giberson
and his gang in a boat. They made the boy a prisoner and
took from him his fowling piece. Then they ordered him
to pilot them to Tuckerton landing. Reaching what was
called "scow landing," they moored the boat and went to
the tavern recently built by Daniel Falkenburg, the first inn
keeper in Little Egg Harbor. As soon as the refugees

reached the tavern they indulged in a drunken revel. Some of the residents sent a messenger to Manahawkin, where there was a company of militia, and informed them of the presence of the refugees in Tuckerton.

A squad of soldiers marched toward the place to capture or disperse the revelers, but a Tory informed the outlaws of their coming and about the time the militia reached Tuckerton the refugees fled to the landing. Seizing their guns they took an advantageous position in the boat. The militia marched down Green Street toward the landing, and as they came near the creek, the refugees poured the contents of their heavily charged guns into the ranks of the militia with such fury and precision that the latter were forced to retreat followed by the outlaws, who pursued them to West Creek. Seeing the retreating militia on the opposite side of the creek, Giberson and his victorious band returned to Tuckerton to go aboard their boat.

When they reached the landing the boat was some distance off. In their absence two of their comrades, who were too drunk to join in the pursuit had become sober enough to unmoor the boat and were paddling the craft down the creek, shouting as their companions came in sight, "We are the boys to hold the boat." The returning outlaws, mistaking them for their enemies, ran along the creek in pursuit. They fired and killed both of the men before discovering that they were of their own gang. After this the refugees returned to the tavern and finished their debauch. Before leaving Tuckerton, Giberson hunted up the boy from whom he had taken the gun, and returned it to him and also presented him with a Spanish dollar.[34]

Thus, in the nineteenth century William Giberson was considered a ruthless outlaw, albeit colorful by virtue of his strength, agility, and daring; in the twentieth century he became almost a Robin Hood figure. One possible reason for this transformation was that in the 1840s, when the legends about Giberson were first written down, some people were alive who had experienced the Revolution first-hand, and Americans were not about to make a hero out of someone who was on the other side. Eighty years later local historians looked back on the Revolution through a nostalgic and romantic filter.

The figure of Joseph Mulliner was similarly transformed. The Mulliners were an English family that came to Little Egg Harbor before the Revolutionary War. Joseph Mulliner left no progeny, but his brother, Moses Mulliner, married Mary Holden, and their children married into the Shourds, Mathis and Ridgway families.[35] In 1781 Joseph Mulliner was arrested for treason, tried by the Burlington County Court of Oyer and Terminer, convicted, and hanged. In his own day he was considered a rogue by both Whigs and Tories, at least according to the *New Jersey Gazette,* which on August 8, 1781 reported on Mulliner's trial as follows:

> At a special court held in Burlington, a certain Joseph Mulliner, of Egg-Harbour, was convicted of high treason, and is sentenced to be hanged this day. This fellow had become the terror of that part of the country. He had made a practice of burning houses, robbing and plundering *all* who fell in his way, so that when he came to trial it appeared that the whole country, both whigs and tories, were his enemies.[36]

Admittedly, the *Gazette* was a Whig newspaper, but there is no evidence that Mulliner, like Giberson, was celebrated in his own day or during the nineteenth century.

In the 1920s, however, local historians began to elaborate upon and romanticize the Mulliner legend. Alfred Heston described Mulliner as "a young man of good address and attractive personal appearance," who "wore an officer's uniform, with a ponderous sword at his side and a brace of pistols in his belt." Heston added a wife and a faithful dog to the portrait. "Mulliner had a dog to whose neck he attached an ingeniously constructed collar, and having trained the dog as a courier, when he wished to communicate with his wife—and through her with some of his absent band—he would write a message, fasten it to the collar and then start the dog across the river." A measure of his newly found legendary status was the fact that it was claimed he was buried in several different places. Heston argued that Mulliner was originally buried at Pleasant Mills but that in 1860 his remains were exhumed and reburied at the Batsto Iron Works. In 1947 local historian Henry Charlton Beck noted that there were claims that Mulliner was "hanged in three places and buried in two."[37]

In the hands of Henry Charlton Beck, Joseph Mulliner became a handsome rogue who would appear unannounced at country taverns and dance with the prettiest girls. Beck's *Forgotten Towns of Southern New Jersey* (1936) contains the following narrative about Mulliner.

It was a stormy night and dark when Joe suddenly appeared, his countenance radiant with rain and his smile revealing two rows of perfect teeth. As someone gasped, "Joe Mulliner," the fiddler stopped and the dancers, moving in the dim-lit parlor of the inn, shuffled uncertainly. Mulliner instantly made a demand that the music go on and that the best-looking girl step out to dance with him.

It was an old demand and the dancers of all the old towns and their stage-stop hotels were used to it. But though buxom damsels afterward boasted a dance with

Mulliner they never willingly answered his invitations. On this occasion there was considerable reluctance. Swains held their girls tight and then Mulliner, whipping out his shooting-iron, gave the men a minute to disappear.

It is a story that has been worn with much handling but not yet has it been called a fable. A timid dancer, a chap perhaps who had been trying for many years to get up the nerve to dance, stayed in the room and defied the gang leader.

"My, my," laughed Mulliner, surprised. "And have all the bold fellows vanished, have all the hawks fled to cover, leaving this chicken-hearted fool among the wenches?"

He of the alleged chicken heart dropped the hand of his partner and swung his own flatly across the face of the intruder. Instead of firing, Mulliner laughed long and loud. Then he shook hands, declaring that so fearless "a little bantam" must have the best girl present. And taking the slapper's partner, he danced a round or two and vanished into the night.[38]

According to Beck, Mulliner was captured while dancing with a girl at one of these taverns.

The most famous incident associated with Joseph Mulliner was the burning of the widow Bates's house, cited by Beck and others. A local history of Pleasant Mills narrated the incident in the following words:

> A widow named Bates owned a small farm near the Forks. . . . She had eight sons, four of whom were serving in the American army; the others, being too young for military duty, assisted her in tilling the little farm which yielded them a comfortable livelihood. . . . Returning

from meeting one Sunday afternoon she found her home in possession of Mulliner's gang, though Mulliner himself was not with them. They had ransacked the house and helped themselves freely to her pigs and poultry and among the plunder made up to be carried away she saw her precious silverware. This was too much and stepping forward the undaunted woman loosed the vials of her wrath and gave the band a terrific tongue lashing.

"Silence madam," said the leader somewhat nettled by her fierce tirade, "silence or we'll lay your d—d house in ashes."

"T'would be an act worthy of cowardly curs like you," snapped the widow, "you may burn my house, but you'll never stop my mouth while there's breath in my body."

One of the refugees entered the house, took a firebrand from the hearth and applied it to the building. With equal promptitude, Mrs. Bates seized a pail of water and dashed it on the rising flame while her boys like sturdy little patriots assailed the enemy with a volley of stones; their pluck, however, availed but little; they were speedily seized and held fast while the mother was dragged across the road and bound to a tree. The house was again fired and the family compelled to look helplessly on until it was entirely consumed. They were then released and the refugees departed with their booty.

The story of Mrs. Bates' misfortune spread far and wide, a host of friends came to her assistance, and in a few days a roomy log house stood on the site of the burned dwelling. Sympathetic neighbors donated furniture sufficient to fit it up snugly and affairs at the little farm went on pretty much as before. A few weeks later Mrs. Bates received the sum of

three hundred dollars from some unknown person and it
was always her belief that Mulliner had taken this means
of atoning in some degree for the misdeeds of his
followers.[39]

The anonymous gift in the above account reconciles the contradiction
of making Mulliner a hero despite the fact that he was on the wrong
side of the Revolutionary conflict.

The account of the burning of the widow Bates's house originates
in fiction, not history. The incident first appeared in an 1855 novel titled
Kate Aylesford, written by Charles J. Peterson of Pleasant Mills. Subtitled
A Story of the Refugees, the novel contains a character, Ned Arrison, who
is based on Joseph Mulliner and whose name may or may not be a
veiled reference to William Giberson. The widow's name may recall the
Bates who captured Giberson. However, Arrison is characterized as
anything but a Robin Hood. He is described as "a short, thick-set man
. . . with a countenance which had never been pleasing, but was now
embruited by intemperance and other vices." He owns a ferocious
bloodhound named Lion, probably the inspiration for the canine ac-
complice in Heston's account of Mulliner. Arrison plots to kidnap the
heroine, Kate Aylesford, who is rescued by the hero, an American
officer named Major Gordon. In the novel the widow Bates's house is
robbed and set afire while she is at Quaker meeting, but Ned Arrison
does not make any restitution. As one character in the novel remarks,
"Nobody but a villain would rob the widow and the orphan. Especially
a soldier's widow. It could only have been the refugees."

One scene in *Kate Aylesford* is set in a country tavern where the
clientele are mostly "boisterous tars" from the privateers in the bay,
along with several countrymen from the small farms in the interior. A
black fiddler plays, while a storm rages outside. A challenge leads to a
contest between a sailor and a countryman in which they dance the

"time honored dance, which is known to the initiated as a 'Jersey Four.'"[40] Similar dancing contests were described in an 1889 guidebook to the New Jersey coast and the Pines.

> In the old days, when the furnaces were in operation, numerous taverns were scattered through the pines. They were called "jug taverns," because their entire stock-in-trade usually consisted of a jug of applejack, out of which, however, the proprietor would pour any liquid refreshment called for, ranging from lemonade to brandy, and even mixed potables. . . . The chief amusements in those days were huckleberry parties in summer and oyster suppers in winter. The latter were held in the taverns and were preceded and followed by dancing. A fiddler enthroned in a chair, which had been elevated on to a table, scraped away at "Hi, Betty Martin," "Camptown Races," and the "Straight Four," dances which were perhaps varied by a "challenge jog" between two experts of the Pines. When the fiddler disappeared under the table, as he invariably did, the girls sang the airs and dancing continued all the same.[41]

The fact that Mulliner became known as a dancer at country inns may have been inspired by the novel or by other descriptions of such dance contests.

It is not unusual for an incident in a novel to become the basis for a legend. Folklorist Henry Glassie observed the same phenomenon in Northern Ireland in reference to the so-called "rapparees," members of the Irish Brigade during the Williamite War, who took to the hills to rob from the rich and give to the poor. Glassie collected tales about two rapparees, Black Francis and Willy Reilly, which originally appeared in a novel titled *Willy Reilly and His Dear Coleen Bawn,* written by William Barleton circa 1855. Glassie's informant, Hugh Nolan, in Glassie's words, "reorganized and recomposed the novel."[42] Similarly, twentieth-century local historians fictionalized the figures of Joseph Mulliner and William Giberson. Generally considered rogues in their own day, they have become heroes today.

In conclusion, as we review the origin of the Pineys legend, we can say with some certainty that the Lenape Indians, Hessian soldiers, and pirates played little, if any, role in the group's lineage. Quakers, Loyalists, privateers, and Pine Robbers, on the other hand, did play a role, though not quite so romantic a one as the legend suggests. While the historical accuracy of the legend is important, it is equally important that people believed it to be factual. Created by local historians in a chain of written, rather than oral, communication, this local-history legend reveals much about the attitudes of outsiders toward the people of the Pines. Over the decades these attitudes underwent changes, and the legend developed and changed accordingly.

At first, the residents of the Pine Barrens were viewed with disdain, mingled with some degree of fear. According to David J. Fowler, such attitudes reflect a negative stereotype of forest dwellers that can be traced back to the seventeenth century in America and even earlier in Europe.[43] In the nineteenth century, as we can see in the pseudoscientific Kallikak study, a strong dose of Social Darwinism was added: the Pineys were viewed as socially, mentally, and morally inferior because of generations of inbreeding and miscegenation. Here the legend took on the racial and social prejudices of the white middle class in the late nineteenth and early twentieth centuries. Starting in the 1920s, local historians toned down the sensational aspects of the legend and took a more romantic and nostalgic approach to the past, as can be clearly seen in the transformation of Joseph Mulliner, the Pine Robber, from a traitor and rogue into a colorful and heroic Robin Hood.

Folklorist Henry Glassie has argued that the distinction between history and legend is ethnocentric: "What we call legends in other societies are precisely what we call histories in our own," and it is "snide" to label "legend" what other people believe about the past and "history" what we believe. He refers to his legend-telling informants in the town of Ballymenone in northern Ireland as "historians."

> There is one past but many histories. We think of one of them—our own—as "history" and others as "folk histories," but they are either all histories or all folk histories. All involve collecting facts about the past and arranging them artfully to explore the problems of the present. Academic historians create a history appropriate to their needs, and the no less serious historians of places like Ballymenone do the same; they create one that suits theirs.[44]

The legend about the origin of the Pineys, however, suggests how important it is to maintain the distinction between documented history and legend. Rather than showing that legend is really history, it suggests that some local history is, in fact, legend.

4

THE "ANGEL DANCERS"

hroughout American history, rumors have surrounded religious sects in America with a wall of distrust and suspicion. Often it is apostates who have provided grist for the rumor mill, yet despite these eyewitness testimonies, the same motifs and themes recur over and over in books, newspaper accounts, and court records pertaining to these so-called "cults."

One case illuminates the others. In the 1890s a small, religious commune was established on the so-called Lord's Farm in the small town of Woodcliff, in Bergen County, New Jersey. The sect was known locally as the "Angel Dancers," a name explained to me in 1968 by Etta Tice Terhune of Park Ridge, New Jersey. She was born in 1891 and grew up on a farm only two miles from the Lord's Farm. Her remembrances from her youth were reinforced by her collection of newspaper clippings on the subject.

COHEN: Well, do you know why they were called the "Angel Dancers"?

TERHUNE: Well, they were supposed to be a religious cult of some kind. And then when they danced—of course, they had to have a name, I suppose.

COHEN: Oh, they danced?

TERHUNE: Yes. Oh, they danced. Sure. In the nude. On the tables. And then they'd make a big cake, and take it right out of the oven, and then when they would get to a certain place on the table, then they'd put their foot in the cake. That showed how religious they were. That's the influence one man could have over twenty or thirty people. Now isn't that ridiculous? In the name of religion. He should have been put in prison.[1]

Emma Mead, also of Park Ridge, was the granddaughter of James Leach, one of the leaders of the local opposition to the Lord's Farm sect. She told me about Mason Huntsman, the leader of the sect, and about its peculiar, religious rites.

MEAD: The Angel Dancers—well, of course, I didn't know them personally. But I've seen them, and I've even been past the house, you know, when they were performing, as they say. But, of course, I don't remember too much what I saw. I was only a little girl. It was a long time [ago], and my grandfather didn't approve of them, you know, and he— Mason, the head fellow up there—had long whiskers and long hair, and grandpa tried to cut it for him. . . . They were [in] Woodcliff Lake. Well, we always called it the Lord's Farm. Up by Fuscoe's Corner. . . . The house is down now. It's only lately they've taken the house down that was the Angel Dancers' house.

COHEN: Why did they call it the Lord's Farm?

MEAD: The Angel Dancers were on the Lord's Farm.

COHEN: Is that what *they* said they were?

MEAD: That's what everybody said. I don't know what *they* said. I never talked to any of them. But I remember going past. And, of course, I tried so hard to see them dancing on the table. . . .

COHEN: Did they dress in any special way?

MEAD: The story is that they were nude. That's the story. Of course, I wouldn't [know] . . . that's why I wanted to see them.

COHEN: Was that the story that was passed around?

MEAD: That's the story that went around. That's the story. I didn't read anything written about them.[2]

Susan Terhune and Beulah Terhune English of Woodcliff Lake were the granddaughters of Cana Watson, another local opponent of the sect. They added the following comments to the story:

ENGLISH: Yes, there was a lot of hanky-panky going on up there.

SUSAN TERHUNE: I heard tell it had no base.

ENGLISH: Well, the children had to come from somewhere.

SUSAN TERHUNE: This was news for this part of the world at that time. It was really news, and it was written up in the *Local*. When people knew about it, they filled in where you didn't read. . . .

COHEN: I heard something about their dancing?

SUSAN TERHUNE: I didn't hear anything about dancing. But there were stories. You can imagine what stories like that let loose in a town like that.

ENGLISH: Everybody who lives around this district got the

word on this. This has been idle gossip for years. Up there, yeah, they had dances up there. But that's all talk too. It was an exclusive cult up there. They used to sing and holler. I doubt that anybody got inside to see them dance, though.[3]

English possessed a photograph of Mason Huntsman. It showed a man with a full white beard and long white hair. Susan Terhune had written the following inscription on the back of the photograph: "Mr. Mason/ Christ of the Lord's Farm (cult)/Woodcliff Lake, New Jersey."

The sect resulted from a religious rift in the Congregational Church of Park Ridge. The first settlers in this part of Bergen County were Jersey Dutch farmers, who moved into the Pascack Valley in the mid-eighteenth century. Park Ridge developed as a nineteenth century railroad suburb, when the Hackensack and New York Railroad (later part of the Erie Lackawanna) was built through the valley in 1870. The Congregational Church of Park Ridge was founded in 1873; its minister was the Reverend Samuel H. Switzer, who, while nominally a Congregationalist, was more sympathetic to the Baptists. Soon doctrinal differences surfaced between Reverend Switzer and James Leach, the superintendent of the Sunday school. Finally, Switzer led a faction that left the Congregational Church and took up quarters in a building formerly used as a private academy. Hard feelings continued for several years. Then, in April 1887, Reverend Switzer and his congregation were notified that they had to vacate "the Academy." Having no other place in which to worship, Reverend Switzer set up a tent on his property and began to hold services in the old-fashioned, camp-meeting tradition.

In May 1887, Reverend Switzer invited an itinerant evangelist named Mason T. Huntsman, also known as Paul B. Mason, to participate in a revival. Huntsman was born in Stroudsburg, Pennsylvania.

When he was eight years old, his parents died, and his family was broken up. He lived with a farmer until he was eighteen and then moved to New York City. "There was not a worse young man in the streets of New York, which I made my place of residence, as I did not hesitate at any depth of sin," he once told a reporter.[4] At the age of thirty-one, he was converted by a sidewalk evangelist. He changed the spelling of his name to M-N-A-S-O-N, after Mnason of Cyprus, described in the New Testament as "an old disciple" (Acts 21:16). At the time he was invited to come to Park Ridge, Mnason was living in Newark.

During the revival, Mnason publicly berated the citizens of Park Ridge. He described the village as "a pest hole of sin" and called the pastor of the local Dutch Reformed Church "a leader of imps" and James Leach "the prince of devils." The residents became increasingly outraged by these verbal assaults: Mnason was pelted with rotten eggs; the services were disrupted; and there was talk of tar and feathers. Matters came to a climax on a Sunday night in July 1887, when a mob of about one hundred people, led by James Leach, broke into the house where Mnason was staying, cut off his beard and long hair, and put him on the first train out of town. Later the leaders of the mob were fined by the county authorities.[5]

In October 1888, Mnason was again in the newspapers. This time it was in regard to charges that during a revival he held in Phillipsburgh, New Jersey, Mnason convinced two young girls, Jennie and Lizzie Ricker, ages fourteen and nine, to leave home. The girls accompanied Mnason to Park Ridge, where they stayed for two weeks with two of Mnason's followers, Mrs. Eliza Berry and Mrs. Jane Howell. Mnason and his followers were arrested and brought to Belvidere, New Jersey to stand trial. He was accused of blasphemy, abduction, and impersonating the Savior. According to the indictment, Mnason, being then and there an imposter in religion, did personate our Savior Jesus Christ and did suffer Lizzie Ricker and Jennie Ricker and diverse other persons being then and there his followers, to pay him, the said Mnason Hountzman [*sic*], divine honor, and did terrify, delude, and abuse Mary A. Ricker [the mother of the girls] and diverse other people by false denunciations and judgments, and did then and there say and declare that he, the said Mnason Hountzman, was Christ of God.[6]

In January 1889, Mnason's case came to trial. He was found guilty, sentenced to six months in the county jail, and fined one hundred dollars plus costs.

When Mnason was released from prison, he returned, not to Park Ridge, but to the Storms family farm in neighboring Woodcliff, New Jersey (today known as Woodcliff Lake). Previously, Mnason had converted the mother of the family, Mae Storms; the son, Garret Storms; and the daughter, Mary Storms; but not the father, Herman Storms. Gradually, a religious commune took shape on the Storms farm, as other followers came there to live. Besides former converts, Eliza Berry and Jane Howell, came new converts, Mary Stewart, Daniel F. Gaines, and John McClintock. The group also took in visitors and orphans.

The members of the commune divided the work equally, using the farm wagon to operate a furniture-moving business and hiring themselves out as agricultural laborers to other farmers in the neighborhood. Members of the sect adopted new names: Mary Storms became "Blandina," after a French martyr at Lyon in the second century A.D.; Garret Storms became "Titus," a disciple of Paul in the New Testament; Mary Stewart became "Thecla," after Thekla of Iconium, who as a convert of St. Paul took a vow of chastity; and Daniel Gaines became "Silas the Pure," who was chosen by the apostles and elders to accompany Paul and Barnabas to Antioch (Acts 15:22). They used the familiar pronouns "thee" and "thou" and addressed each other as "sister" and "brother." They adhered to plainness of dress and wore their hair uncut, in accordance with their interpretation of Biblical law. They were pacifists and vegetarians, abstaining from butter and eggs as well as meat, and they drank no coffee or tea. They also took a vow of absolute chastity.

Soon rumors began to spread about the sect. It was said that they did not believe in marriage and that they did not observe Sunday as the day of rest. But the most sensational report concerned what their neighbors called the "Angel Dance." According to one local newspaper:

> Neighbors claim that twice a month they hold a dance in one of the rooms, which they call the "Angel's Dance," to drive away the devil. . . .
>
> Strange stories are told of the ceremonies with which "God's people" conduct their secular [sic] religious observances, and many tales are told of the wild orgies that have been held at the farm.
>
> Lately, it is alleged they have been indulging more frequently than usual in the "Angel Dance." It is claimed that the participants appeared arrayed as Venus, and that they stand in a circle grasping a blanket between them. While chanting a sacred hymn they give the devil a "blanket tossing."[7]

These rumors prompted a neighbor to file a complaint against the sect for violating the Sunday blue laws. Mary Storms and Mnason were in Newark at the time, but three members of the sect—Eliza Berry, Jane Howell, and Garret Storms—were arrested and brought before Justice John C. Wortendyke. Storms and Berry pleaded guilty and were fined three dollars each, but they refused to pay their fines and were sentenced to four days in the Hackensack jail. Howell was discharged for lack of evidence.

When Mary Storms and Mnason returned from Newark, they too were arrested and brought before Justice Wortendyke. Mnason explained that he was like a Seventh-Day Adventist in that he kept the Sabbath on Saturday, but he denied that he had husked corn on the Sunday in question. Justice Wortendyke discharged both defendants. According to the newspapers, "When asked if it were true that he and his followers held an 'angel dance' occasionally, when all disrobed in the parlor and waved a blanket to drive away the Devil, Mnason said that he would not deny it."[8]

In April 1893, the entire sect was arrested on the accusation that they had conspired to cheat and defraud Herman Storms of his farm. In addition, it was charged

> that the conspirators denied, ridiculed and curse all regular religion and religious customs; recognize no Sabbath and set up a false God of their own, declaring that he the said Mnason to be the only true and living God. In consequence the household of Herman Storms has been turned into a petty and grinding despotism under the dogmatic rule of Huntsman T. Mnason, aided and abetted by his said co-conspirators, wherein unseemingly [sic] revelry often occurs and disorder reigns, and the laws of society, religion and state are defied and reviled to the scandal of the neighborhood and great injury to public morals.[9]

Bail was set at one thousand dollars, but the accused refused to post it, and they were imprisoned in the county jail in Hackensack to await indictment by a grand jury. Since the grand jury did not convene until September, the sect members spent the entire summer in jail. Justice W. B. Smith of Park Ridge later told a reporter, "For five years I have been trying to break up this free-love band, but could not get anyone to make a complaint, but my efforts were not in vain. . . . I will do what I can to keep them in jail or drive them to some other quarter."[10]

While in jail Mnason wrote a letter to the editor of the county newspaper, seeking to defend himself against the accusation that he had violated the Sabbath. He argued that the true Sabbath, according to Scripture, was the seventh day of the week, but he rendered "custom to whom custom is due" by observing the Sabbath on Sunday, "for all things are lawful for me, but not expedient." He also denied that he thought of himself as God.

> Moreover, the word of the Lord God of Israel came unto me, saying, "Write this unto the people, that by the devil through the papers and gossip of the people, who know nothing about Mnason of a personal knowledge, not having a personal talk with him, have deluded the people by making them believe that Mnason is God, which is an untruth and a falsehood in the evil hearts of wicked people.[11]

In September the grand jury met and indicted the defendants, but no mention was made of any conspiracy to defraud Herman Storms. Instead, the charges were changed to keeping a disorderly house, breaking and destroying crockery and other property belonging to Herman Storms, and burning three of his Bibles. All of the defendants pleaded not guilty, and the trial date was set for October.

At the trial Herman Storms was the chief witness for the prosecution. His testimony was printed almost verbatim in the newspapers.

> Herman Storms, at whose farm at Woodcliff the angel dancers lived, testified as to the length of time they had been there—some five or six years, some only a short time. "They carried on nights and made it extremely unpleasant for me. They broke furniture and crockery and destroyed food. I was eating supper one night when Mnason told Howell to get up on the table and walk around. She did so. I had some bread and butter and preserves on my plate. She stepped on my food. I took her arm and pulled her off the table. Then my daughter, Mary, Mnason, and others got on the table and all walked around. There was a fresh baked cake, which Jane Howell said she made, setting on the table. They all stepped on it as they passed. My wife said she didn't approve and they made her clean up the mess."[12]

Herman Storms was cross-examined by Mnason, Daniel Gaines, Jane Howell, and Mary Storms, who defended themselves without the aid of legal counsel. In the opinion of one reporter, they weakened Herman Storms's testimony considerably, because he seemed uncertain about many details.

In the afternoon session Herman Storms was recalled to the stand. The newspaper account continued:

> He testified that Mnason said that the Bible was nothing but a dime novel. That Mary Stewart, Jane Howell, and Mary Storms had burned some Bibles belonging to him. Mnason shouted at the time, "Glory, it is all right. I am the greatest. I have all power." He had seen what they called the angel dance. The women all had hold of a blanket and

were dancing around the room, the men and women all
singing and shouting, "Glory," "Hallelujah," "Amen," and
carrying on.[13]

During the cross-examination Mary Storms noted that at the time the
blanket dance allegedly took place, the defendants were in the
Hackensack jail.

The next day Mary Storms took the stand. She refused to swear
an oath on the Bible. In her testimony she flatly denied that she had
walked on the table, burned Bibles, or broken dishes. As for the
infamous dance: "I deny that I ever engaged in or saw what has been
called a blanket dance."[14]

Despite the defendants' denials of any wrongdoing, the jury
returned a verdict of guilty. Judge James Van Valen sentenced Mnason
and Jane Howell, as the leaders of the sect, to one year in the state
prison in Trenton. The others were taken before the court as a group
and told that they could go free, if they promised to leave the county
or, in the case of the Storms family members, to return home and "live
as a family." At first Mary Storms refused, but after a few more weeks
in jail, she capitulated and was released.

Only one champion came forward to defend Mnason and his
followers publicly. He was Alfred P. Smith, an invalid African American who published an amateur newspaper, *The Landscape,* out of his
home in Saddle River, New Jersey (see chapter 2). Smith eloquently
spoke out against the injustice of the trial: "The case will furnish a
curious chapter in the history of intolerance and the ignorant and
mendacious jumble of a charge on which these people were committed, if preserved, will be read by future generations with wonder at the
ignorance, bigotry, and perversion of law, to gratify religious rivalry
and spite, in Park Ridge in 1893."[15] Smith lived only a mile from the
Lord's Farm, and he visited it on several occasions, once staying for an

entire week. Taking on the New York City newspapers, Smith tried to refute the rumors about the sect.

> Some of the papers have again had one of their erup-
> tions concerning the people they name "Angel Dancers."
> The editor of *The Landscape,* being personally acquainted
> with all of those thus called, knows what he is talking
> about when he has anything to say about "Angel Dancers."
> We have seen them at their own fireside and elsewhere,
> and all we have seen has won from us the highest admira-
> tion and respect.[16]

In 1895 Smith wrote that "people are recognizing the worth of the so-called 'Angel Dancers' concerning whom 'fake' newspapers and filthy imaginations have woven so many romances, which many at one time were credulous enough to believe."[17] This proved to be wishful thinking.

When he was released from prison, Mnason returned to the Lord's Farm, but the legal harassment continued. In August 1899, members of the sect were arrested again: Mnason and Garret Storms were charged with assault upon two girls, Emily and Lucy Lamb, ages fourteen and thirteen; and John McClintock and Mary Storms were charged with maintaining a disorderly house. These charges were based on an affidavit, signed by the girls' mother, Mrs. Annie Lamb of Bristol, Massachusetts, at the urging of a reporter from the New York *World.* Mrs. Lamb charged that Mnason and Garret Storms had a mysterious power over her daughters, that they taught the girls to hate their parents, and that shocking immoralities were practiced on the Lord's Farm.

During the trial, in October 1899, it was brought out that Mrs. Lamb voluntarily had brought her daughters to live on the Lord's

Farm. The jury returned a verdict of not guilty for the charges against Mary and Garret Storms and John McClintock and found Mnason guilty, but recommended mercy in sentencing. The judge, however, set aside the verdict against Mnason on the grounds that the evidence did not warrant his conviction. Lucy and Emily Lamb were retained in prison as potential witnesses in a possible new trial. Their parents tried to get them released, but they could not afford the bail, which had been set at one thousand dollars. Finally, after seven months in jail with no new trial, the Lamb girls were released in the custody of a county freeholder. The reason for this arrangement, it was explained, was because the girls wanted to return to the Lord's Farm, the authorities would not let them go back, and it took time to find a "suitable" home for them.

The ownership of the Lord's Farm changed hands several times. In March 1898, Mary Storms transferred the title to her share of the farm to John McClintock. He kept this share for three and a half years, until November 1902, when he deeded it back to Garret and Mary Storms. The next month Mary Storms transferred her share to her brother. In January 1903, Garret Storms rented the dwelling, outbuildings, and land to Mnason at a yearly rent of five thousand dollars, the lease containing a provision that Garret and his sister would be entitled to use and occupy the premises. On January 7, 1904, Garret Storms deeded the farm to Mnason with the stipulation that Mnason would retain title only during the natural life of Garret Storms.[18]

On January 12, 1904, at the age of thirty-eight, Mary Storms died of what was described by her physician as "a dropsical complaint." Within weeks of her death, speculation grew among the neighbors as to whether she had left a will. But the farm was not Mary's to dispose of, Mnason being in legal possession of it. Here is one newspaper account:

> People for several miles around Woodcliff are anxiously
> awaiting to learn whether Miss Mary Storms, surnamed
> "Blaudina," [sic] of the "Angel Dancers," left a will. This
> anxiety is due to the fact that this young woman who died
> two weeks ago remarked that the Lord thought she should
> give the farm to Huntsman T. Mnason, the leader of the
> band. No will has been recorded in Hackensack. The fact
> that Mnason served a year in State prison in 1893 for
> conspiring to cheat Herman Storms out of his farm adds
> interest to the situation. Mnason has the entire Storms
> family under his influence.[19]

In fact, Mnason had been convicted of keeping a disorderly house and
destroying property, not of conspiring to defraud Storms.

Then, in February 1905, John McClintock committed suicide. It
was reported that he had been despondent over the death of Mary
Storms. There were now left only four members of the sect on the
Lord's Farm: Mnason, Garret Storms, Mae Storms, and a new recruit
named Robert William Johnson. The newspapers ceased to take an
interest in the farm, although Mnason and perhaps some of his followers continued to live there for several more years. Then, in April
1910, Mnason deeded the farm back to Garret Storms, evidently after a
falling-out between them. This seems to have marked the end of the
Lord's Farm experiment in communal living.[20]

About ten years after Mnason left the Lord's Farm, a writer
named Theodore Schroeder came across him in the main reading
room of the New York Public Library, where he was wont to sit,
writing down his inspirations. Schroeder described Mnason as "a
chubby, bustling, picturesque little man . . . [who] had a ruddy face,
almost Irish in its appearance. Long white hair that came well down

over his shoulders was accentuated by a long, flowing white beard and a broad-brimmed hat."[21] Schroeder again encountered Mnason in New York City at a service in the Church of the Living God, an African American congregation. Desiring to learn more about this strange man, Schroeder invited Mnason to visit his home in the country.

After hours of conversation, Schroeder attempted a paraphrase of Mnason's beliefs. Schroeder inserted parenthetic comments and psychological interpretations, but except for these interpolations, the text was approved by Mnason, and it constitutes the most complete statement of the beliefs that guided the Lord's Farm.

When questioned about the relationship between himself and God, Mnason replied as follows:

> I just gave myself up more and more to the inner voice and by practice I gradually came thereby to recognize myself as being possessed of the inner Christ. He is here [pointing to his own breast]. His is the word that was heard and the Word was made flesh in me. He is the essential me. . . .
>
> By living the life of God [inner voice], I am in fact God and am so recognized. . . .
>
> When you see me, you see the Father. I am the outward manifestation of God, absolutely and eternally. I am in God and God is in me. We are one within the body that is called Mnason. The gold and silver and cattle on a thousand hills are God's, are mine.[22]

Schroeder noted that the only books Mnason read were the Bible; the writings of George Fox (1624–1691), the founder of the Society of Friends; and the writings of Madame Jeanne Bouvier de la Motte Guyon (1648–1717), a French Catholic mystic who was persecuted for her unorthodox religious beliefs. This is revealing in light of Mnason's own persecution and because the above passage sounds much like the Quaker doctrine of the "inner light," that is, the spark of the divine in every being created by God. This Quaker-inspired belief in the "inner light" may have been the basis for the rumor that Mnason's followers worshiped him as God.

Schroeder questioned Mnason also about the Bible and got this response:

> When I saw by reading what Jesus, Paul and the rest were, I said, "This is what I am going to be." After that was obtained, the Bible was no more than any other book. It was a dead letter. One must come into Christ to get divine life. The Bible is now no good to me. I am the Word made flesh in the likeness of a man, and the form of a servant. I am before the Bible. In the beginning was the Word, and the Word was God. Whosoever have God within themselves and acknowledge this in their every activity are the Word.[23]

And so, like the Quakers, Mnason stressed direct inspiration rather than the Bible. This was probably the basis for the charge that he and his followers destroyed Bibles.

Mnason commented too on the concept of love and the institution of marriage:

> He that is born of God is a spirit. Children of this world marry and are given in marriage. I am not of this [physical] world. They that shall be accounted worthy to belong to that other [spiritual] world [by being in harmony with the mandates of the spirit through the inner voice] neither marry nor are given in marriage, but are angels of God and love-children of the resurrection. When you are in God, you are in love. . . .

A spirit will never marry. It doesn't have to. The spiritual man always has plenty of companions [in fantasy] and can live marriage inwardly [psychological homo- or auto-eroticism?]. Here there is a spiritual union like that of the flesh, but not in the flesh. This union is spiritual oneness. . . .

The satisfying presence of God removes fleshly desires [psychic eroticism is a sufficiently satisfying presence]. We must recognize that God within and thereby convert human affection into divine love. There is no other kind of love.[24]

If one disregards Schroeder's gratuitous, psychological interpretations one gets from this passage a clear explanation of the practice of celibacy on the Lord's Farm. It was based on a neo-Platonic dualism of body and soul. The rumors about sexual promiscuity on the Lord's Farm represent a complete reversal of Mnason Huntsman's teachings on celibacy and sexual abstinence.

What makes the case of the Angel Dancers especially intriguing is that similar rumors were spread about other celibate religious communes. For example, Johann Conrad Beissel, the founder of the Protestant monastic sect at Ephrata, Pennsylvania, was said to be so attractive to women that they would leave their husbands to join his sect. One such woman was Maria Sauer, wife of Christopher Sauer, the publisher of the first German Bible in America. Sauer published a pamphlet in which he accused Beissel of portraying himself as Christ. An apostate named Ezekiel Sangmeister also wrote an exposé of the Ephrata Society, in which he accused Beissel of being "a drunkard, an incubus, and a lustful hypocrite who had sexual relations with the sisters in the sect and contracted venereal disease."[25]

The most famous communal sect to inspire such rumors was the

Shakers, located in upstate New York, western Massachusetts, and Ohio. Today, the Shakers are celebrated for their elegantly simple style of furniture, but in the early nineteenth century they too were the victims of their neighbors' suspicion. The historian Edward Deming Andrews wrote:

> The wildest stories, originating in some instances by the New Light ministers themselves, circulated about the Shakers. They were accused not only of parting husband and wife and ruining families, but of deliberately planning under the cloak of piety, to steal people's land and property. It was rumored that each Believer thought himself a Christ, that the Shakers consequently saw no need for Bibles, that they boasted they would never die.[26]

It was said that Mother Ann Lee, the founder of the Shakers, was worshiped as the female embodiment of Christ, and there is some basis in fact that she was so regarded by her followers. It was also said that the sect held children captive, an accusation that remains unproven. In August 1810, a mob attacked the Shaker community at Union Village, Ohio, demanding the release of children allegedly held captive there, although the children in residence insisted that they did not want to leave. Similar incidents occurred in 1813, 1817, and 1824.

Although the Shakers believed in absolute chastity, they were accused of sexual promiscuity. In 1810 Colonel James Smith published two pamphlets charging that the Shakers castrated the males in the sect, danced naked, and had promiscuous debauches. An apostate named Thomas Brown made similar accusations, which were cited by Timothy Dwight, the president of Yale College, in the following passage from his *Travels in New England and New York:*

> Antecedently to the year 1793, the men and women on a variety of occasions danced naked.

On a particular occasion William Lee [Anne Lee's brother], after a drunken frolic, professed that he had a revelation which required himself and about twenty of the brethren to dance naked. Mother Ann came to the door and insisted on coming into the room. She then attempted to get in at the windows. William prevented her. She then forced the door open with a stick of wood. William met her at the door, and Ann struck him with her fists. William said, "The smiting of the righteous is like precious ointment." Her blows, however, were redoubled in such rapid succession that he at length ceased from answering them with this text; and, finding the blood running from his face, he replied with his fist, and knocked her almost down. The brethren then parted them; and, after some violent threatening on both sides, the rejoicing ended.[27]

Of course, the Shakers denied these accusations. A Shaker sister named Mary Hocknell was quoted in 1812 about how such stories might have originated.

Because the brethren pulled off their coats, or outside garments, to labour, or as they would call it, dancing; and in the warm weather the sisters being lightly clothed, they would report we danced naked. And you know how apt the ignorant and vulgar part of mankind are to misrepresent what they see. If one told they danced part naked, or with but few clothes on, another in telling the story, would leave out the part, or few, and so it was reported that we danced naked.[28]

Her explanation might apply as well to the rumors circulated about the "Angel Dancers."

Intellectual historians have viewed communitarianism, that is, the movement to establish utopian communities, as reflecting a central concept in American thought: that in the "New World" it was possible to rebuild society from scratch. Wrote historian Arthur Bestor:

> Rarely has society been so open and free as to make plausible a belief that new institutions might be planted, might mature, and might reproduce themselves without being cramped and strangled by old ones. In America in the early nineteenth century, however, men and women believed that they could observe new institutions in the making, and they were confident that these would develop without check and almost without limit.[29]

Bestor noted that communitarianism in America had its roots in the radical Protestant sects of Europe. During the seventeenth and eighteenth centuries American communitarianism was associated with religious sects, such as the Puritans, the Moravians, and the Shakers. In the early nineteenth century, religious communitarianism evolved into secular socialism, inspiring such experiments as the Oneida Colony in New York State, New Harmony in Indiana, Brook Farm in Massachusetts, and the North American Phalanx in New Jersey. However, after the Civil War, according to Bestor, communitarianism went into decline "because social patterns had become so well defined over the whole area of the United States that the possibility no longer existed of affecting the character of the social order merely by planting the seeds of new institutions in the wilderness."[30]

Folklore, however, provides a different understanding of the relationship between communitarianism and American society, especially in regard to religious sects. In recent years folklorists have begun to study rumor. Most of this research has focused on the so-called "urban belief legends," which are modern-day rumors like the "Vanishing

Hitchhiker," but the approach also can shed light on rumors of the past.[31] The example of the "Angel Dancers" is informative for several reasons. Not only does it document the process of rumor formation in regard to one small, religious sect, but there is a striking similarity to the rumors spread about other religious sects, most notably the Ephrata Society and the Shakers. Whether or not there is a factual basis for these rumors, it is important to understand that rumors like these tend to be spread about religious sects in any case, regardless of real evidence. The vulnerability of sects to scandalous rumor refutes the alleged compatible relationship between communitarianism and American society. While some American intellectuals may have been sympathetic to efforts to remake society, there is evidence in the folklore surrounding small religious communes that the rest of the population was not.

5

REFLECTIONS ON AMERICAN ETHNICITY

he ends of centuries tend to be times of summing up. It was in 1893, at the World's Congress of Historians held in conjunction with the Columbian Exposition in Chicago, that historian Frederick Jackson Turner delivered his seminal essay, "The Significance of the Frontier in American History." He began by citing the announcement in 1890 by the Superintendent of the United States Census of the official closing of the American frontier.[1] Turner's essay crystallized a recurrent theme in American thought—that American culture was the product of the frontier—and his frontier thesis influenced several generations of historians that followed. Today, much of the frontier thesis has been refuted, and the advent of the New Social History, women's history, and ethnic history has fragmented historical thinking. There is no longer a commonly accepted paradigm, like the

frontier thesis, to unite American historical studies, although there may well be one implicit in the new approaches. It is my contention that any attempt to create a new synthesis would have to involve the significance of ethnicity in American history.

In 1992 the nation celebrated the quincentennial of Columbus's arrival in the Americas. Overshadowed by this celebration was another anniversary: the opening in 1892 of the federal immigration station on Ellis Island. All commemorations are symbolic, and historical analysis based on commemorative observances can be more misleading than illuminating. It is all too easy, and perhaps misguided, to suggest, as Turner did, that the closing of the frontier was a turning point in American history, or that it was in any way related to the opening of Ellis Island.

Ethnicity has been an important factor from the beginning of American history. In a sense, ethnicity explains more about how American culture was shaped than the frontier does. Conceived by Turner as either a line moving westward or as an area of supposed free land, the frontier is an ethnocentric concept, for it is limited to an Anglo-American perspective on history. It may be more accurate to see the frontier as the place where Europeans, African Americans, and Native Americans came into contact with each other. Many of the cultural traits usually associated with the frontier were in fact ethnic. Three examples are the log cabin, the covered wagon, and the cowboy. Research by folklorists and cultural geographers has shown that the log cabin was not an indigeneous product of the American frontier. It was a fusion of Scandinavian and Germanic log construction techniques with English and Scotch-Irish floorplans. First introduced in the Delaware Valley, log construction diffused though the Appalachian Valley into the Trans-Appalachian West, following the routes of migration.[2] The covered wagon, or Conestoga wagon, as it was sometimes called, is derived from northern European freight and farm wagons found in western Germany and the Netherlands and adopted by the English from the Dutch. Thus, there were German, Dutch, and English prototypes for the famed "prairie schooners" of the American West.[3] The cowboy was not, in fact, Anglo-American, but a product of cattle-ranching traditions introduced to the Americas by the Spaniards. The *gaucho* of Argentina, the *llanero* of western Venezuela and eastern Colombia, and the *vaquero* of Mexico and the American cowboy all were part of the same Spanish ranching complex.[4]

Instead of viewing the settling of North America in the ethnocentric terms of the western migration of English-speaking people, the frontier may better be visualized as the boundary between settlements of several European groups (the French in Canada, the Spaniards in New Spain, the Dutch in New Netherland, the Swedes in New Sweden, the English in the British colonies), several Native American groups (the eastern woodland, the southeastern, the plains, the southwestern, the Pacific northwestern), and several West African groups (the Yoruba, the Kongo, the Dahomean, the Mande). The interaction among these peoples resulted, in the words of environmental historian Andrew W. Crosby, in a "Columbian exchange" that reshaped the diet, the language, the music, the dance, not just of America, but of the world.[5]

Before proceeding, we should distinguish between immigrant groups and ethnic groups. Immigration is only one of several ways that an ethnic group comes to reside in a particular place. It refers to the voluntary act of leaving one's country of birth and moving to another country to live and work. Clearly, the immigration model does not apply to most African Americans and Native Americans. With the exception of those people of African ancestry who have immigrated to the United States from South America, the Caribbean, or Africa (whom the census, incidentally, lists as black, not African American), most African Americans were brought to America involuntarily as slaves. Native Americans, of course, were here already when the first Europeans arrived. The current theory is that their ancestors migrated from Asia to the Americas about fifteen thousand years ago across a land bridge that once spanned the Bering Straits. Thus, Native Americans exemplify two other ways by which ethnic groups have come into existence: that is, by migration and by conquest.

There are those who argue that African Americans and Native Americans should not be considered ethnic groups, but rather racial groups. Through the 1930s American sociologists continued to refer to immigrant groups as races. For example, both Jews and Italians were called "races" at one time. It was not until World War II, in reaction to the Nazi theory of an "Aryan master race," that scholars began to distinguish between race, linguistic group, and ethnic group.[6] Within its definition of ethnicity the *Harvard Encyclopedia of Ethnic Groups* includes regional groups (Southern Appalachian Mountain People, Southerners, Yankees) as well as religious groups (Jews, Eastern Catholics, Mormons, Muslims).[7] I would argue that race, nationality, language, region, kinship, or religion may help define an ethnic group, but not always; they are not synonymous with ethnicity. Blacks may be African American, Afro-Cuban, Jamaican, or Haitian; Jews may be Sephardic or Ashkenazic; Hispanics may be Cuban, Colombian, Dominican, or Puerto Rican. For example, race does not distinguish Afro-Cuban from African American; nationality does. But race does distinguish Afro-Cuban from Cuban. The point is that it makes sense to use the concept of ethnicity, when any of the above concepts alone does not explain the group identity. Thus, I would not call Southerners or Appalachian Mountain People or Yankees ethnic groups; nor would I call blacks, Jews, or WASPs ethnic groups. However, I would call African Americans, Ashkenazic Jews, and the English ethnic groups. Ethnicity is only one kind of cultural identity. There are also regional cultures such as the Pinelands (see chapter 3), religious cultures such as the Angel Dancers (see chapter 4), and cultures that combine region with race and ethnicity such as the Afro-Dutch (see chapter 2). There is also a national culture, or popular culture, which may have some ethnic origins, but is no longer the exclusive possession of any one ethnic group. It is not that all culture is ethnic, but that ethnicity is a major factor in shaping American culture.

Ethnicity is dynamic. Ethnic identities emerge and change. Immigrants become ethnics, a process which is manifested in the emergence of a sense of group identity. Many nineteenth-century immigrants identified with the town or region from which they came, not the country. (In fact, the country, as a political entity, may not have existed when they left.) The Poles identified with Warsaw or Galicia, the Italians with Sicily or Naples, the Germans with Hanover or Bavaria. It was only after they settled in America that a "national" identity emerged. In some cases, even the name by which the group is presently known is a recent coinage. The term "Ukrainians," for example, was not used commonly until the twentieth century, the group which it designates being previously known as Ruthenians or Little Russians, terms which they today dislike. Often the identity that emerged in the United States was a composite of traits drawn from different regions of the old country. For example, the Ukrainian American ethnic identity combines the woodcarving tradition from the Carpathian Mountains, the music and dance tradition of the Cossacks, and the embroidery and costumes of the eastern province of Poltava.[8] My own research on the Dutch in New Netherland indicates that more than half their ancestors were not from the Netherlands. They came from places adjacent to the Low Countries, and became culturally Dutch because this was the dominant culture of the region. My work with the Ramapo Mountain People shows that a group that originated as free blacks who were culturally Dutch is now asserting a Native American identity and gradually having that identity accepted by their neighbors and the newspapers, if not the Bureau of Indian Affairs, as an Indian tribe.[9]

The problem of defining ethnicity is complicated by changes in the accepted meaning of the word. The Greek word *ethnos,* which means "nation" or "race," was used in the Old and New Testaments as the equivalent of "the nations (or peoples)" (that is, Gentiles or non-Jews). The English word "ethnic," from the Middle Ages through the eighteenth century, meant "pertaining to nations not Christian or Jewish," or "Gentile, heathen, or pagan."[10] In other words, ethnic meant foreigners—them, not us. This usage continued into the twentieth century. In *Yankee City,* the classic 1941–1945 study of immigrants in Newburyport, Massachusetts, sociologist W. Lloyd Warner defined an ethnic as "any individual who considers himself or is considered to be a member of a group with a foreign culture and who participates in the activities of the group."[11]

The argument that immigrants should not be considered foreigners can be traced back to Walt Whitman's declaration that America is "a nation of nations." This notion that all Americans are ethnics is related to the concept of "cultural pluralism," a term coined by the Jewish American philosopher Horace M. Kallen in the 1920s and popularized by the Slovenian American writer Louis Adamic in the 1930s. Rather than distinguishing between foreigners and "true" Americans, the proponents of cultural pluralism suggested that everyone who came to settle in America was an American. In the late 1930s, cultural pluralism became part of the official ideology of the New Deal and found expression in New Deal cultural programs, especially the WPA Federal Writers' Project.[12]

Although conformity eclipsed cultural diversity from the late 1940s through the early 1960s, cultural pluralism came into vogue again during the Ethnic Revival of the 1970s and 1980s, which has been marked by a renewed interest in tracing one's ethnic roots, the growth of multicultural and bilingual programs in the secondary schools, the organization of ethnic studies programs at colleges and universities, and the celebration of ethnic cultures in festivals and other events. Yet there is a basic difference between the ideal of cultural pluralism of the 1920s and 1930s and the Ethnic Revival of the 1970s and 1980s. The former was a reaction to the nativism that prompted the immigration restrictions of the twenties; the latter, in large part, a reaction to the Black Pride movement of the 1960s. The ideal of cultural pluralism was based on a vision of ethnic harmony, while an undercurrent of ethnic conflict runs through the Ethnic Revival of recent years, as each group promotes its own political agenda (bilingual education, Afrocentrism, Native American rights, Holocaust studies). This is not to say that ethnic conflict and ethnic politics did not exist until the 1970s. On the contrary, the emergence of both the Irish and the Poles as ethnic groups in America was integrally linked to the desire of Irish and Polish Americans to promote national independence for their homelands.[13]

Some historians and sociologists see ethnic groups as subcultures within a predominantly white, Anglo-Saxon, Protestant America. They use the term "ethnic" to mean "minority," as distinct from a vague construct called "mainstream" American culture. While it is true that there is a popular culture that cuts across regional, class, religious, racial, and ethnic divisions, this popular culture is not the property of any single ethnic group. Nevertheless, there have always been those who wished to define American culture in terms of their own region, class, religion, or ethnicity. The frontier thesis, for example, may be considered Frederick Jackson Turner's effort to define America in terms of the West, the region from which he came.

It has been customary to refer to the United States as predominantly WASP, because American law and government are derived from the experience of the British colonies. Historian David Hackett Fischer argues, in addition, that the population of the United States in 1790 was predominantly British in origin.[14] There are two problems with his findings. First, he tallies only whites; African Americans, who constituted approximately 19.3 percent of the population in 1790, are completely overlooked. Second, he treats the English, the Scots, and the Irish as a single ethnic group. When one factors out the non-English people who came from the British Isles, but who were English neither in language nor culture, and factors in African Americans, it turns out that only about 49.2 percent of the population of the United States in 1790 was of English extraction. Thus, the English were the largest single ethnic group—followed by the African Americans (19.3 percent); the Irish, from both Ulster and Eire (7.8 percent); the Germans (7 percent); the Scots (6.6 percent); and the Dutch (2.6 percent). But the English constituted a plurality, rather than a majority, of the total population.[15]

Some scholars persist in distinguishing between the so-called "old" immigrants (that is, the Irish, Germans, and Chinese who came to the United States in great numbers between 1840 and 1880) and the "new" immigrants (the eastern and southern Europeans who came between 1880 and 1930).[16] There are several problems with this periodization, but most notable is the definition of "new" immigration. To term an immigration that ended in 1930 as "new" may have made sense at one time, but certainly not today. Furthermore, the period since World War II has seen a whole new wave of immigration from yet other parts of the world. The immigrants who have come since the Immigration Act of 1965 may be the real "new" immigrants, but so may those who have come since 1980, a date that also marks a shift in the places of origin. The problem will not go away as long as we cling to the terms "old" and "new."

I would like to suggest a different periodization, one not solely concerned with immigration, and with British North America, but

with the "peopling," by whatever means, of the North American continent.[17] I suggest four major periods: (1) the pre-Columbian migration
of the ancestors of Native Americans across the Bering Straits and their
dispersal throughout North America, (2) the migration of Europeans
and Africans, mostly as indentured servants and slaves during the
colonial period, from about 1500 to the end of the slave trade in the
United States in 1808, (3) the period between 1820 and 1930, during
which European immigrants were attracted to the United States by the
related developments of industrialization and urbanization, and (4) the
period between World War II and the present, marked by suburbaniz-
ation, a gradual shift to a postindustrial economy, and (after 1965) the
arrival of a great number of immigrants from Latin America, the
Caribbean, and Asia. These consecutive waves of settlement have
changed the overall makeup of the population of the United States.

In 1500, when Europeans first settled in the Western Hemisphere, the Native American population stood at about 90 to 112
million, of which about 10 to 12 million lived in North America. They
were divided into different language families (Algonquian, Iroquoian,
Siouan) and culture areas (eastern woodland, southeastern, plains,
southwestern, and Pacific northwestern). Unlike other major populations that settled North America, after contact with Europeans, the
population of Native Americans decreased drastically because of war
and disease, until it reached a low point of approximately 490,000 in
1930. The most recent estimate of the total Indian population in the
United States, taken from the 1990 census, is 1.8 million, although this
figure may be a bit suspect, because since 1980 the United States
Census Bureau has relied on self attribution of ethnic and racial identity. There are a number of groups in New Jersey and elsewhere
throughout the United States that identify themselves as Indian, although they cannot prove more than a minimal Indian ancestry, if that
(see chaps. 1 and 3). Between 1980 and 1990 the number of people that

identify themselves as Indian in New Jersey increased 78.3 percent, jumping from 8,394 to 14,970.[18]

The subsequent migrations to North America from Africa and Europe overwhelmed the declining population of Native Americans. In what historian Bernard Bailyn has called "one of the greatest events in recorded history," an estimated 50 million people from Europe and Africa came to North America between 1500 and the present day. During the seventeenth century alone, more than 378,000 emigrants left England for the Western Hemisphere, of whom 155,000 came to North America. Most of them were indentured servants, who were recruited because of the chronic labor shortage that existed in colonial America. The other solution to the labor shortage was slavery. Between 1500 and 1870 approximately 11 million Africans were forcibly brought to the Americas through the Atlantic slave trade, of whom about 500,000 were brought to British North America, until the termination of the slave trade in the United States in 1808.[19]

The ban on the importation of slaves to the United States marked the close of the second period of immigration and the beginning of the third, which witnessed the replacement of indentured and slave labor (after 1865) with free labor in the South and West and an industrial and urban workforce in the Northeast. In 1790 only 5.1 percent of the population of the United States was urban; by 1920, this figure had swollen to 51.2 percent. The percentage was even higher in the Northeast: by 1880, 50.8 percent of the total population of this region was urban; by 1920, 75.5 percent. The great industrial cities of the Northeast were truly immigrant cities. In 1910 first- and second-generation immigrants comprised 78 percent of New York City's population, 77 percent of Chicago's, and 74 percent of Boston's. More and more people left the countryside to take up residence in the cities, and there was a corresponding change in occupational patterns. In 1800, 73.7 percent of the total workforce was engaged in farming. By 1910 farm workers constituted only 30.9 percent of the civilian work force, white collar workers 21.4 percent, and manual and service workers (that is, factory and domestic labor) 48.2 percent.[20] This last category was the one in which most of the immigrants found jobs.

The number of people who immigrated during this third period was phenomenal. Between 1820 and 1930 almost 38 million immigrants came to the United States, that is, almost ten times the total population of the United States in 1790. During the peak decade, between 1901 and 1910, 8.8 million arrived, a number unmatched either before or since. Ninety-two percent of the immigrants between 1821 and 1930 came from Europe. The traditional view is that the so-called "old" immigrants in the early nineteenth century were primarily German and Irish, while the "new" immigrants in the late nineteenth century came primarily from eastern and southern Europe. The Germans and the Irish did indeed constitute the majority of the immigrants for the early period, but the eastern and southern Europeans remained a minority until the first decade of the twentieth century. While 57.8 percent of the total number of immigrants between 1821 and 1880 came from Ireland or Germany; only about 47.5 percent of the total number between 1881 and 1930, came from eastern and southern Europe. However, for the peak decade between 1901 and 1910 approximately 68.8 percent came from eastern and southern Europe. A large number of the immigrants who came during this third period eventually returned to their homelands, the rates of return varying from ethnic group to ethnic group: 87.4 percent for Bulgarian/Montenegrin/Serbians, 66.1 percent for Rumanians, 53.7 percent for Greeks, 45.6 percent for Italians, 4.3 percent for Jews. This period of mass immigration was brought to a close in the 1920s by a series of laws that established quotas restricting the number of eastern and southern Europeans who could enter the United States. The discouraging economic conditions of the Great Depression also had their effect. During the period from 1931 to 1940 only about 528,000 immigrants came into the United States.[21]

The period since the end of World War II saw a major shift in the population from cities to suburbs, a decline in heavy industry, and the gradual establishment of yet another pattern of immigration. Beginning in 1950 the United States Census Bureau began to enumerate the population in what they termed Standard Metropolitan Areas, which were later renamed Standard Metropolitan Statistical Areas. These were defined as a county or group of contiguous counties that is socially and economically integrated and contains at least one city with a population of fifty thousand or more. The Standard Metropolitan Statistical Area differed from an urbanized area in that the former was not built up throughout and might contain rural areas in close proximity to developed ones. The shift of population from cities to suburbs is reflected in the fact that in 1950 there were only fourteen Standard Metropolitan Areas and these accounted for less than 30 percent of the total population of the United States, while in 1990 there were thirty-nine, and a little more than half (50.2 percent) the nation was concentrated within them.[22]

At the same time, there was a decrease in the percentage of the work force engaged in factory labor as compared to the period from 1808 to 1930. In 1988, 69.7 percent of the civilian labor force was classified as managerial, professional, technical, sales, service, or administrative support; 27.4 percent as precision production, craft, repair, operators, fabricators, and laborers; and only 3 percent as farming, forestry, or fishing.[23]

As the flow of immigration resumed after World War II, preferential treatment was given to refugees, first from the displaced persons camps in Europe and then, from the late 1950s through the 1980s, from Communist countries, such as Hungary, Cuba, and Vietnam. In

1965 the United States enacted a major revision in its immigration laws, altering the previous quota system and thereby opening the door to non-European immigrants. At the same time, the law gave preferential treatment to certain skilled workers needed in a postindustrial economy. The new policies soon became evident in the immigration statistics. Between 1941 and 1988, about 16 million immigrants came to the United States. Almost half of those who came between 1941 and 1965 (49.5 percent) came from Europe, but an increasing percentage came from Latin America and the Caribbean (25 percent in all). Only 5.8 percent came from Asia. In the decade from 1971 to 1980, by contrast, only 18 percent of the total number of immigrants came from Europe; the percentage from Latin America and the Caribbean increased to 34 percent; and Asian immigration surged dramatically, accounting for 36 percent of all new arrivals to the U.S. And the trend has continued. According to the 1990 census, Asians are the fastest-growing immigrant group in the country, having increased by 108 percent between 1980 and 1990, followed by Hispanics, who increased 53 percent during the same period.[24]

Ethnicity has had an important impact on the local, regional, and national levels of American culture and society. The ethnic neighborhood is one of the most visible signs of ethnicity in America, as was noted by Robert E. Park and his students and colleagues at the University of Chicago in the 1920s. They observed that immigrants in Chicago tended to cluster together in "colonies" or "ghettos," which were segregated, residential enclaves. These ethnic neighborhoods underwent a process that the University of Chicago sociologists termed "succession," as more recent immigrant groups replaced earlier ones.[25] However, as historian Humbert S. Nelli has shown, despite the high visibility of one ethnic group in these neighborhoods, rarely was the neighborhood the residence of a single ethnic group, nor did a single ethnic group even constitute a majority of the population. Typically, one or two ethnic groups comprised a plurality of the population and stamped their identities on the neighborhood.[26]

This pattern can be seen in Newark, New Jersey in the Ironbound or Down Neck neighborhood, so named because it is bounded by railroad trestles and by a necklike curve in the Passaic River. In 1860, the largest foreign-born group in the Fifth Ward (the Ironbound) was the Irish, comprising 37 percent of the total population, followed by the Germans (20 percent). By 1910, the ethnic makeup of the neighborhood had changed, but the largest group still constituted only a plurality of the population. In that year, the most populous group was born in Italy (comprising 11.7 percent of the total), followed by 11.3 percent born in Russia, and 7.7 percent in Austria. Poles would have been included in the numbers for Russia and Austria, because Poland at that time did not exist as a separate country. The 1980 census, which listed ethnic ancestry rather than country of birth, indicated yet another change in the neighborhood. The largest ethnic group now was the Portuguese, who accounted for 36.6 percent of the population, followed by the Spaniards (14.7 percent), and the Puerto Ricans (9.8 percent). Some Italian and Polish residents (8 percent and 4.4 percent, respectively) remained in the neighborhood as well.[27]

African Americans are the one major exception to this pattern of single ethnic groups constituting only a plurality in ethnic neighborhoods. For them, residential segregation in northern, urban neighborhoods has been steadily increasing.[28] In the city of Newark, blacks constituted only 5 percent of the population of the Third Ward in 1850. By 1940, in the midst of the Great Migration of African Americans from the South to northern cities that commenced during World War I, blacks constituted 63.2 percent of the population of the Third Ward. By 1980, blacks constituted 75 percent or more of the population in fifteen of Newark's census tracts, and 90 percent or more in seven others. This unprecedented degree of urban residential segregation is unmatched by any other ethnic group. Even Hispanics, who, like blacks, are often targeted by prejudice, live in more diversified neighborhoods.[29]

Not only are different ethnic groups clustered in special neighborhoods within cities, but each city has a distinctive ethnic makeup, an important component of its identity and character. For example, the largest foreign-born population in Milwaukee in 1920 was German (33.1 percent of the total foreign-born population); in Boston it was Irish (23.5 percent); and in New York it was Russian and Lithuanian (24 percent), approximately 80 percent of which was Jewish.[30] Thus, the association of Boston with the Irish, Milwaukee with the Germans, and New York with the Jews has some basis in the actual distribution of ethnic populations.

Ethnicity is not solely an urban phenomenon. One of the lesser-explored dimensions of American ethnic history is rural ethnicity. In 1911 *Recent Immigrants in Agriculture,* a report of the United States Senate's Immigration Commission, noted that in 1900, 21.7 percent of all foreign-born breadwinners were employed in agriculture. The largest number of foreign-born farmers were German, but there were also Norwegians, Swedes, Italians, Poles, Portuguese, Bohemians, and Japanese. In southern New Jersey alone, there were significant agricultural populations of Germans, Italians, and eastern European Jews.[31] To this day, many Italians continue to be engaged in agriculture in South Jersey.

In the 1950s and 1960s sociologists Herbert J. Gans and Will Herberg argued that class or religious identities eclipsed ethnic identity in the suburbs, but the overall pattern we see emerging since the 1960s indicates that ethnicity continues strong in suburbia.[32] The 1990 census shows that, like urban ethnic neighborhoods, certain suburban communities have become associated with particular ethnic groups. For example, in Belleville, New Jersey, (a suburb of Newark), people either wholly or partly of Italian extraction constituted 78.6 percent of the total population; in South River, New Jersey, 40 percent of the population is either wholly or partly of Polish descent; and in the Jersey shore community of Spring Lake, those of Irish or partly Irish descent constituted 92 percent of the population. Middle-class blacks also have moved out of the inner cities into the suburbs. The largest suburban black concentration in New Jersey was in Plainfield, where African Americans constituted 63 percent of the total population over the age of seventeen. In the post-World War II suburban community of Willingboro, New Jersey, which was the Levittown studied by Herbert Gans, blacks constituted 52.4 percent of the adult population.[33]

The differential distribution of ethnic groups also has influenced regional identities. In 1860, two-thirds of the Irish in the United States lived in New England or the Mid-Atlantic States, mostly in cities, and about half the Germans in the country lived in the Midwest, mostly on farms. The 1980 census showed that 79 percent of Polish Americans lived in the Northeast and Midwest, in what some people have termed the "Polka Belt"; 53 percent of African Americans lived in the South; 77 percent of Japanese Americans in the West; and 73 percent of Puerto Ricans in the Northeast.[34]

On the national level, shifts in the sources of immigration have changed the overall make-up of the American population. According to the 1990 census, the total population of the United States was 248.7 million. Of this total 12.1 percent listed themselves as black, 9 percent as Hispanic, 2.9 percent as Asian or Pacific Islander, and 0.8 percent as American Indian. Hispanics are quickly challenging blacks as the largest minority group, and American pluralism continues to mean that no one ethnic group comprises more than a plurality of the population.

To those who argue that ethnicity undermines the national culture of the United States, I would note that many so-called national cultural traits originated in ethnic cultures. I already have mentioned the log cabin, the covered wagon, and the cowboy, all of which have ethnic origins. Many of the foods we think of as American were originally ethnic. Consider such Native American foods as corn (maize), the tomato, and chili peppers; the German sausage, which became the American hot dog; the Italian pizza; the Jewish bagel; and the Mexican taco—all of which have become typically American, as measured by their appearance on the menus of franchise restaurants around the country. The American language, which is the spoken word as opposed to that artificial construct termed "standard English," has incorporated expressions from a variety of languages spoken by American ethnic groups. Consider such African American expressions as "boogie-woogie," "jive," "jazz," "rock and roll," and "rap"; the Dutch "stoop," "cookie," and "hook" (for a point of land); the Spanish "vamoose," "calaboose," "buckeroo" (from *vaquero*); the German "kindergarten," "delicatessen," and "nix" (for veto); the Chinese "kowtow"; the Yiddish "klutz"—and so on.[35] American music has also been shaped by ethnic traditions, from the African American blues and spirituals to the Scotch-Irish ballads and fiddle tunes, which together represent the twin fountainheads of American folk and popular music. To this mix has been added Cajun, Tex-Mex, polka, salsa, and zydeco music. Similarly, dance in America has been invigorated by African American buck dancing, Celtic American step dancing (which is the grandparent of American square and clog dancing), as well as by the numerous dance traditions that have come from Latin America (tango, samba, mambo, cha-cha, conga). And finally, let us not forget the many ethnic festivals, including both those that originate in the traditions of a single-group, like Saint Patrick's Day, now celebrated by Irish and non-Irish alike, and the currently ubiquitous multiethnic festivals that have become so popular since the 1970s. Clearly, ethnic traditions not only continue to thrive in the United States, but help to shape the popular culture of the nation.

I am not suggesting that ethnicity is the only, or even the most important, force in explaining the direction of American history. Race, class, religion, gender, and region have also played their parts, and although these variables are all related to ethnicity, they can also function independently of it. Certain events in American history, such as the Civil War, for example, may best be explained by factors other than ethnicity, such as race or region or constitutional issues.

There are those today who disapprove of ethnic diversity, or multiculturalism as its most recent manifestation. Whatever one calls it and whether or not one approves of it, ethnicity is a fact of life in America and has been from the beginning. But what is the future of ethnicity in America? As the world enters a post-Cold War era and ethnic conflicts in eastern Europe and the Middle East seem to be tearing nations apart, what will be the effect of ethnic diversity in the United States? I do not adhere to the Pollyanna view of those cultural pluralists who think that all Americans need do is attend multiethnic festivals and sample unfamiliar foods and all tensions will be resolved. The history of ethnic conflict in the United States should make it impossible for anyone to imagine that ethnicity has always been a force for peace and understanding or that interethnic hostilities can be easily allayed. However, what makes ethnicity in the United States different than in most other countries is that no one ethnic group has constituted more than a plurality of the total population. I do not mean to deny that there has been domination of various sectors of the population in American history, such as the domination of blacks by whites, of Native Americans by Europeans, of women by men. In the last analysis, however, James Madison's insight about factions applies to American ethnicity: namely, that the United States is sufficiently large and sufficiently diverse that no one ethnic group has achieved an enduring dominance. To rephrase Madison's dictum, in the United States of America we behold a pluralistic remedy for the diseases most incident to a pluralistic society.

NOTES

Introduction

1. Robert Hughes, *Amish; the Art of the Quilt* (New York: Alfred A. Knopf, 1990), pp. 16, 21.

2. Everett V. Stonequist, *The Marginal Man: A Study in Personality and Culture Conflict* (1937; reprint, New York: Russell and Russell, 1961); Fredrik Barth, *Ethnic Groups and Boundaries: The Social Organization of Culture Difference* (Bergen-Oslo and London: Universitets Forlaget and George Allen and Unwin, 1969).

3. John McPhee, *The Pine Barrens* (1967; reprint, New York: Ballantine Books, 1971).

4. Burt Feintuch, ed., *The Conservation of Culture: Folklorists and the Public Sector* (Lexington: University of Kentucky Press, 1988); Ormond H. Loomis, *Cultural Conservation: The Protection of Cultural Heritage in the United States* (Washington, D. C.: Library of Congress, 1983).

5. Mary Hufford, *One Space, Many Places: Folklife and Land Use in New Jersey's Pinelands National Reserve . . .* (Washington, D.C.: American Folklife Center, Library of Congress, 1986).

6. David Steven Cohen, *The Folklore and Folklife of New Jersey* (New Brunswick: Rutgers University Press, 1983), pp. 39–50.

7. Molefi K. Asante, *The Afrocentric Idea* (Philadelphia: Temple University Press, 1987).

8. Sterling Stuckey, *Slave Culture: Nationalist Theory and the Foundations of Black America* (New York: Oxford University Press, 1987).

9. Orlando Patterson, *Ethnic Chauvinism: The Reactionary Impulse* (New York: Stein and Day, 1977).

10. Arthur M. Schlesinger, Jr., *The Disuniting of America* (New York and London: W. W. Norton, 1992).

Chapter 1. Emergent Native American Groups in New Jersey

1. James Clifford, *The Predicament of Culture: Twentieth-Century Ethnography, Literature, and Art* (Cambridge: Harvard University Press, 1988), pp. 3–11, 14, 17.

2. For two other views of the Mashpee trial, see Jack Campisi, *The Mashpee Indians: Tribe on Trial* (Syracuse: Syracuse University Press, 1991) and Paul Brodeur, *Restitution: The Land Claims of the Mashpee, Passamaquoddy, and Penobscot Indians of New England* (Boston: Northeastern University Press, 1985). For the genealogical record on the Ramapo Mountain People, see David Steven Cohen, *The Ramapo Mountain People* (1974; reprint, New Brunswick: Rutgers University Press, 1986).

3. Helen C. Rountree, *Pocahontas's People: The Powhatan Indians of Virginia Through Four Centuries* (Norman and London: University of Oklahoma Press, 1990), p. 3; J. Dyneley Prince, "An Ancient New Jersey Indian Jargon," *American Anthropologist* 14 (1912): 510; Herbert C. Kraft, *The Lenape: Archaeology, History, and Ethnography* (Newark: New Jersey Historical Society, 1986), pp. xvii-xviii.

4. "Population Distribution for New Jersey by Race and Hispanic Origin: 1990 and 1980," *United States Department of Commerce News,* January 1991, Table 1; "Census Finds Many Claiming New Identity: Indian," *New York Times,* March 5, 1991, p. A16.

5. Fredrik Barth, *Ethnic Groups and Boundaries: The Social Organization of Culture Difference* (Bergen-Oslo and London: Universitets Forlaget and George Allen and Unwin, 1969), pp. 17–18, 22–24; Paul

Robert Magocsi, "Ukrainians," in Stephen Thernstrom, ed., *Harvard Encyclopedia of American Ethnic Groups* (Cambridge and London: Belknap Press of Harvard University Press, 1980), pp. 200–210; Clifford, *The Predicament of Culture,* pp. 278, 289, 294–295.

6. Cohen, *The Ramapo Mountain People,* pp. 25–59, 97–101, 111–116.

7. C. A. Weslager, *The Nanticoke Indians—Past and Present* (Newark, Del.; London and Toronto: University of Delaware Press and Associated University Press, 1983), pp. 254–255.

8. Richard R. Wright, Jr., "The Economic Condition of Negroes in the North: III. Negro Communities in New Jersey," *Southern Workman* (1908): 385–386.

9. William Steward and Rev. Theophilus G. Steward, *Gouldtown: A Very Remarkable Settlement of Ancient Date* (Philadelphia: J. B. Lippincott, 1913), pp. 52–54.

10. Robert G. Johnson, "Memoir of John Fenwick, Chief Proprietor of Salem Tenth, New Jersey," *Proceedings of the New Jersey Historical Society* 4 (1849): 53–89.

11. Ibid., pp. 62–63.

12. Frank G. Speck, "The Nanticoke Community of Delaware," Museum of the American Indian, Heye Foundation, *Contributions* 2 (1915): 2.

13. C. A. Weslager, *Delaware's Forgotten Folk: The Story of the Moors and Nanticokes* (Philadelphia: University of Pennsylvania Press, 1943), pp. 16, 17.

14. Speck, "The Nanticoke Community," pp. 2–3.

15. Weslager, *Delaware's Forgotten Folk,* pp. 3–4.

16. Quoted in Weslager, *Delaware's Forgotten Folk,* pp. 34–35.

17. Ibid., pp. 36, 78; Speck, "Nanticoke Community," p. 9n.

18. Christian F. Feest, "Nanticoke and Neighboring Tribes," in William Sturvesant, gen. ed., *Handbook of the North American Indian,* vol.

15, Bruce G. Trigger, ed., *Northeast* (Washington, D.C.: Smithsonian Institution, 1978), p. 240; Weslager, *Delaware's Forgotten Folk,* p. 43.

19. Weslager, *Delaware's Forgotten Folk,* pp. 58, 69, 74–75.

20. Thomas Jefferson, *Notes on the State of Virginia* (1785; reprint, New York: Harper Torchbooks, 1964), pp. 91–92.

21. Rountree, *Pocahontas's People,* pp. 187–196.

22. Chief Roy Crazy Horse, *A Brief History of the Powhatan Renape Nation* (Rancocas, N.J.: Powhatan Renape Nation, 1986), pp. 3, 25.

23. Rountree, *Pocahantas's People,* pp. 218–224.

24. Weslager, *Delaware's Forgotten Folk,* p. 95.

25. Weslager, *The Nanticoke Indians,* pp. 223–224.

26. Vanessa Brown and Barre Toelken, "American Indian Powwow," *Folklife Annual* (1988): 46–68; Gertrude Prokosch Kurath, "Pan-Indianism in the Great Lakes Tribal Festivals," *Journal of American Folklore* 70 (1957): 179–182; Weslager, *Nanticoke Indians,* pp. 13–20; Hazel W. Hertzberg, *The Search for an American Indian Identity: Modern Pan-Indian Movements* (Syracuse: Syracuse University Press, 1971).

Chapter 2. Afro-Dutch Folklore and Folklife

1. Thomas F. De Voe, *The Market Book, Containing a Historical Account of the Public Markets in the Cities of New York, Boston, Philadelphia, and Brooklyn, etc.* (1862; reprint, New York: August M. Kelley, 1970), 1: 344.

2. Frank Tannenbaum, *Slave and Citizen: The Negro in the Americas* (New York: Afred A. Knopf, 1947); Eugene D. Genovese, *The World the Slaveholders Made: Two Essays in Interpretation* (New York: Vintage Books, 1969); Lawrence W. Levine, *Black Culture and Black Consciousness: Afro-American Folk Thought from Slavery to Freedom* (Oxford, London, and New York: Oxford University Press, 1977); Edgar McManus, *A History of Negro Slavery in New York* (Syracuse: Syracuse

University Press, 1966); Joyce D. Goodfriend, "Burghers and Blacks: The Evolution of a Slave Society in New Amsterdam," *New York History* 59 (1978): 125–144; William Stuart, "Negro Slavery in New Jersey and New York," *Americana Illustrated* 16 (1922): 347–367.

3. James A. Rawley, *The Transatlantic Slave Trade: A History* (New York and London: W. W. Norton, 1981), p. 386; Giles R. Wright, *Afro-Americans in New Jersey: A Short History* (Trenton: New Jersey Historical Commission, Department of State, 1988), pp. 19, 21; Peter O. Wacker, "The Changing Geography of the Black Population of New Jersey, 1810–1860: A Preliminary View," *Proceedings of the Association of American Geographers* 3 (1970): 174; idem., *Land and People: A Cultural Geography of Preindustrial New Jersey* (New Brunswick: Rutgers University Press, 1975), pp. 190–191; Francis D. Pingeon, *Blacks in the Revolutionary Era,* New Jersey's Revolutionary Experience, no. 14 (Trenton: New Jersey Historical Commission, 1975), p. 6; idem, "Slavery in New Jersey on the Eve of the Revolution," in William C. Wright, ed., *New Jersey in the American Revolution: Political and Social Conflict,* rev. ed. (Trenton: New Jersey Historical Commission, 1974), p. 57.

4. Melville J. Herskovits, *The Myth of the Negro Past* (1941; reprint, Boston: Beacon Press, 1958), p. 123.

5. Rawley, *The Transatlantic Slave Trade,* pp. 329, 331–332; Tannenbaum, *Slave and Citizen,* p. 6; Wright, *Afro-Americans in New Jersey,* p. 16.

6. Rawley, *The Transatlantic Slave Trade,* pp. 82–83; quoted in David Steven Cohen, *The Ramapo Mountain People* (1974; reprint, New Brunswick: Rutgers University Press, 1988), pp. 25, 27; Goodfriend, "Burghers and Blacks," p. 138.

7. Rawley, *The Transatlantic Slave Trade,* pp. 386–388; Jacob Judd, "Frederick Philipse and the Madagascar Trade," *New York Historical Society Quarterly* 55 (1971): 354–374.

8. Rawley, *The Transatlantic Slave Trade,* pp. 387–388, 403, 407,

411–412.

9. James B. H. Storms, *A Jersey Dutch Vocabulary* (Park Ridge, N.J.: Pascack Historical Society, 1964), n.p.

10. Cohen, *The Ramapo Mountain People;* John Dyneley Prince, "The Jersey Dutch Dialect," *Dialect Notes* 3, part 4 (1910): 460, 468.

11. Dell Hymes, ed., *Pidginization and Creolization of Languages* (Cambridge: Cambridge University Press, 1971), p. 3.

12. Storms, *A Jersey Dutch Vocabulary;* William Nelson and Austin Scott, eds., *Documents Relating to the Colonial History of the State of New Jersey,* 1st ser., vol. 12, *Newspaper Extracts,* vol. 2, *1740–1750* (Paterson: Call Printing and Publishing Co; Trenton: State Gazette Publishing Co., 1895–1917), p. 102; 1st ser., vol.25, *Newspaper Extracts,* vol. 6, *1766–1767,* p. 141; 2d ser., vol. 5, *Newspaper Extracts,* vol. 5, *1780–1782,* p. 25.

13. Robert A. Hall, Jr., *Pidgin and Creole Languages* (Ithaca: Cornell University Press, 1966), pp. 17–18.

14. Prince, "The Jersey Dutch Dialect," p. 467.

15. Robert Farris Thompson, *Flash of the Spirit: African and Afro-American Art and Philosophy* (New York: Vintage Books, 1983), pp. 103, 108, 113, 115.

16. Alexander Coventry, Diary, July 1783-August 1789, New York State Library MSS, Albany, N.Y., p. 211.

17. J. L. Dillard, *Black Names,* Contributions to the Sociology of Language, ed. Joshua A. Fishman, no. 13 (The Hague: Mouton, 1978), pp. 22–23, 91.

18. Elizabeth L. Gebhard, *The Parsonage between Two Manors: Annals of Clover Reach* (Hudson, N.Y.: Bryan Printing Co., 1909), pp. 224–225.

19. Coventry, Diary, p. 108.

20. "Pinkster Ode, Albany, 1803," *New York Folklore Quarterly* 8

(1952): 35; quoted in Alice Morse Earle, *Colonial Days in Old New York* (New York: Empire State Book Co., 1926), pp. 196–198.

21. Gertrude P. Kurath and Nadia Chilkovsky, "Jazz Choreology," in Alan Dundes, ed., *Mother Wit From the Laughing Barrel: Readings in the Interpretation of Afro-American Folklore* (1973; reprint, New York and London: Garland, 1981), pp. 107–108; Marshall Stearns, *The Story of Jazz* (1955; reprint, New York: Mentor Books, 1958), pp. 39–40, 43–45; "Gravel Springs Fife and Drum," documentary film (Memphis, Tenn.: Center for Southern Folklore, 1971).

22. *Diary of William Dunlap* (New York: New York Historical Society, 1929–1931), 1: 65.

23. James Fenimore Cooper, *Satanstoe* (1845; reprint, New York: G. P. Putnam's Sons, n.d.), pp. 66–67.

24. Gabriel Forman, *Antiquities of Long Island* (New York: J. W. Bouton, 1874), pp. 265–266.

25. A. J. Williams-Myers, "Pinkster Carnival: Africanisms in the Hudson River Valley," *Afro-Americans in New York Life and History* 9 (1985): 16; Sterling Stuckey, *Slave Culture: Nationalist Theory and the Foundations of Black America* (New York:Oxford University Press, 1987), pp. 80–83; Shane White, "Pinkster in Albany, 1803: A Contemporary Description," *New York History* 70 (1989): 195; idem, "Pinkster: Afro-Dutch Syncretization in New York City and the Hudson Valley," *Journal of American Folklore* 102 (1989): 72–74. For the viewpoint that the Americanization of the Dutch came earlier, during the Great Awakening, see David Steven Cohen, *The Dutch-American Farm* (New York: New York University Press, 1992); Gerald F. De Jong, *The Dutch Reformed Church in the American Colonies* (Grand Rapids, Mich.: William B. Eerdman, 1978); David Evan Narrett, "Patterns of Inheritance in Colonial New York City, 1664–1775: A Study in the History of the Family" (Ph.D. diss., Cornell University, 1981). For the continued exis-

tence of a black community in New York City, see Joyce D. Good-friend, *Before the Melting Pot: Society and Culture in Colonial New York City, 1664–1730* (Princeton: Princeton University Press, 1992), pp. 111–132.

26. Nelson, *Documents,* 1st ser., 12: 102; John Hosey Osborn, *Life in the Old Dutch Homesteads* (Paramus, N.J.: Highway Printing Co., 1967), p. 156; Charles A. Huguenin, "The Legend of Martense's Lane in Brooklyn," *New York Folklore Quarterly* 21 (1956): 112–118; Charles H. Kaufman, "An Ethnomusicological Survey Among the People of the Ramapo Mountains," *New York Folklore Quarterly* 23 (1967): 125–126.

27. Quoted in David Steven Cohen, *The Folklore and Folklife of New Jersey* (New Brunswick: Rutgers University Press, 1983), p. 64.

28. Levine, *Black Culture and Black Consciousness,* pp. 190–191; Robert B. Winans, " 'Sadday Night and Sunday Too': The Uses of Slave Songs in the WPA Ex-Slave Narratives for Historical Study," *New Jersey Folklore* 7 (1982): 10–15.

29. Leroy K. Irvis, "Negro Tales From Eastern New York," *New York Folklore Quarterly* 11 (1955): 165.

Chapter 3. The Origin of the "Pineys"

1. Jack McCormick and Richard T. T. Forman, "Introduction: Location and Boundaries of the New Jersey Pine Barrens," in *Pine Barrens: Ecosystem and Landscape,* ed. Richard T. T. Forman (New York, San Francisco, and London: Academic Press, 1979), p. xxxvi; John W. Harshberger, *The Vegetation of the New Jersey Pine-Barrens: An Ecological Investigation* (Philadelphia: Christopher Sower Co., 1916), pp. 15–16; New Jersey Pinelands Commission, *Comprehensive Management Plan for the Pinelands National Reserve (National Parks and Recreation Act, 1978) and the Pinelands Area (New Jersey Pinelands Protection Act, 1979)* (New Lisbon, N.J.: The [Pinelands] Commission, 1980), plate 1.

2. Herbert Norman Halpert, "Folktales and Legends from the New Jersey Pines: A Collection and Study" (Ph.D. diss., Indiana University, 1947), 1:15–16.

3. Quoted in John W. Sinton, ed., *Natural and Cultural Resources of the New Jersey Pine Barrens* (Pomona, N.J.: Stockton State College, 1979), p. 165; David Steven Cohen, *The Folklore and Folklife of New Jersey* (New Brunswick: Rutgers University Press, 1983), p. 22.

4. Tom Ayres, "Pinelands Cultural Society: Folk Music Performance and the Rhetoric of Regional Pride," in Sinton, *Natural and Cultural Resources of the Pine Barrens,* pp. 226–227; Angus Gillespie, "Folk and Hillbilly Music in the Pines: Gladys Eayre and the Pineconers' Repertoire," in Sinton, p. 236.

5. Quoted in Martin B. Williams, "The Spiritual Needs of Shamong and the Pine Barrens in 1866," *New Jersey Folklore* (1979): 5–6.

6. W. F. Mayer, "In the Pines," *Atlantic Monthly* 3 (1859): 566–568.

7. Quoted in Harry Bischoff Weiss, *The History of Applejack or Apple Brandy in New Jersey from Colonial Times to the Present* (Trenton: New Jersey Agricultural Society, 1954), pp. 122–123; Francis B. Lee, "Jerseyisms," *Dialect Notes* 1 (1893): 332; Julian Ralph, "Old Monmouth," *Harper's New Monthly Magazine* 89 (1894): 337.

8. Elizabeth S. Kite, "The 'Pineys': Today Morons; Yesterday Outcasts, 'Disowned' Friends, Land Pirates, Hessians, Tory Refugees, Revellers from Joseph Bonaparte's Court at Bordentown, and Other Sowers of Wild Oats," (New Jersey State Library, Trenton, N.J.; typescript reprinted in *The Survey,* October 4, 1913); Henry H. Goddard, *The Kallikak Family: A Study in the Heredity of Feeblemindedness* (New York: Macmillan, 1913); Robert L. Dugdale, *The Jukes: A Study of Crime, Pauperism, Disease and Heredity* (New York: G. P. Putnam's Sons, 1877); J.

David Smith, *Minds Made Feeble: The Myth and Legacy of the Kallikaks* (Rockville, Md.: Aspen Systems Corp., 1985), pp. 83–113.

9. Kite, "The Pineys," pp. 9–10; quoted in Halpert, "Folktales and Legends from the New Jersey Pines," 1: 11–12.

10. Mayer, "In the Pines," p. 566.

11. Ralph, "Old Monmouth," p. 337.

12. Kite, "The Pineys," pp. 4, 7, 10–11.

13. Henry Charlton Beck, *Forgotten Towns of Southern New Jersey* (1936; reprint, New Brunswick: Rutgers University Press, 1961), pp. 9–10.

14. Goddard, *The Kallikak Family*, p. 18.

15. John McPhee, *The Pine Barrens* (1967; reprint, New York: Ballantine Books, 1971), pp. 23–27, 36–38.

16. See, David Steven Cohen, *The Ramapo Mountain People* (New Brunswick: Rutgers University Press, 1974) and Gary B. Mills, *The Forgotten People: Cane River's Creoles of Color* (Baton Rouge: Louisiana State University Press, 1977).

17. Edward McM. Larrabee, *Recurrent Themes and Sequences in North American Indian-European Culture Contact*, Transactions of the American Philosophical Society, vol. 66, part 7 (Philadelphia: American Philosophical Society, 1976), pp. 4, 5, 13, 15, 17.

18. Samuel Smith, *The History of the Colony of Nova-Caesaria, or New Jersey* . . . (1765; reprint, Spartanburg, S. C.: Reprint Co., 1966), p. 442n; Robert Steven Grumet, "'We Are Not So Great Fools': Changes in Upper Delawaran Socio-Political Life, 1630–1758" (Ph.D. diss., Rutgers University, 1979); Frank H. Stewart, *Indians of Southern New Jersey* (Woodbury, N.J.: Gloucester County Historical Society, 1932), pp. 82–86.

19. Robert J. Sim and Harry B. Weiss, *Charcoal-Burning in New Jersey from Early Times to the Present* (Trenton: New Jersey Agricultural Society, 1955), p. 17; U.S. Bureau of the Census, New Jersey, 1880,

Monmouth County (manuscript), Division of Archives and Records Management, New Jersey Department of State, Trenton, N.J., p. 15; Carter G. Woodson, *Free Negro Heads of Families in the United States in 1830* (Washington, D.C.: Association for the Study of Negro Life and History, 1925), pp. 75–76, 81; Frances D. Pingeon, *Blacks in the Revolutionary Era,* New Jersey's Revolutionary Experience, no. 14 (Trenton: New Jersey Historical Commission, 1975), p. 20.

20. *Mt. Holly Herald,* April 15, 1932, p. 3; Stewart, *Indians of Southern New Jersey,* p. 88; U.S. Bureau of the Census, New Jersey, 1880, Burlington County (manuscript), p. 13; Agreement by Brotherton Indians to Sell Land at the Brotherton Reservation, January 15, 1802, Division of Archives and Records Management, New Jersey Department of State, Trenton, N.J.; Ann Roberts, Will, August 7, 1894, Division of Archives and Records Management, New Jersey Department of State, Trenton, N.J.

21. *Early Recollections and Life of Dr. James Still, 1812–1885* (1877; reprint, Medford, N.J.: Medford Historical Society, 1971), pp. 19–20.

22. Woodson, *Free Negro Heads of Families,* pp. 76–77, 81; C. A. Weslager, *Delaware's Forgotten Folk: The Story of the Moors and Nanticokes* (Philadelphia: University of Pennsylvania Press, 1943).

23. Theophilus G. Steward and William Steward, *Gouldtown: A Very Remarkable Settlement of Ancient Date* (Philadelphia: J. B. Lippincott, 1913), pp. 49, 62–63.

24. Lelah Ridgway Vought, *Ridgway-Ridgeway Family History* (n.p.: published by the author 1973), pp. 6, 7, 11; Leah Blackman, *A History of Egg Harbor Township . . .* (Trenton: Trenton Printing Co., 1963), pp. 178, 194–195, 199, 331; Edwin Salter, *A History of Monmouth and Ocean Counties* (Bayonne: E. Gardner and Son, 1890), pp. xxi-xxii; Beck, *Forgotten Towns of Southern New Jersey,* pp. 19–23.

25. Halpert, "Folktales and Legends from the New Jersey Pines," 1:199.

---

26. *Hessische Truppen im Amerikanischen Unabhangigkeitskrieg* (Marburg, Germany: Archivschule Marburg Institut fur Archivwissenschaft, 1972); George P. Griffiths, *Clevenger, Pioneers and Descendants* (Baltimore: Gateway Press, 1980), pp. 15, 16–17, 20, 22; Irwin Gladstone Sooy, "Genealogical Records of the Sooy Family" (typescript, 1941), Burlington County Historical Society MSS, Burlington, N.J., pp. 1–2; Sooy Family Data, Division of Archives and Records Management, New Jersey Department of State, Trenton, N.J., Liber BBB, p. 417; Bozarth Family, Burlington County Historical Society MSS, Burlington, N.J.; Ralph Beaver Strassburger, *Pennsylvania German Pioneers* . . . (Baltimore: Genealogical Publishing Co., 1966), 1: 279; Heinrich Rembe, "Emigration Materials from Lambscheim in the Palatinate," in *Rhinelands Emigrants; Lists of German Settlers in Colonial America*, ed. Don Yoder (Baltimore: Genealogical Publishing Co., 1981), p. 101.

27. William Nelson, ed., *Documents Relating to the Colonial History of the State of New Jersey*, 1st ser., vol. 11, *Newspaper Extracts*, vol. 1, *1704–1739* (Paterson: Press Printing and Publishing Co., 1894), pp. 43–44, 62–63; John Franklin Jameson, *Privateering and Piracy in the Colonial Period* . . . (New York: Macmillan, 1923), pp. ix, xic, 190–257; William Westerman, "New Jersey Pirate Lore: Captain Kidd," *New Jersey Folklore* 8 (1983): 2–5.

28. Quoted in Arthur D. Pierce, *Smugglers' Woods: Jaunts and Journeys in Colonial and Revolutionary New Jersey* (New Brunswick: Rutgers University Press, 1960), p. 19. See also James H. Levitt, *For Want of Trade: Shipping in New Jersey Ports, 1680–1783* (Newark: New Jersey Historical Society, 1981), pp. 18–20.

29. Pierce, *Smugglers' Woods,* p. 52.

30. David J. Fowler, "'Nature Stark Naked': A Social History of the New Jersey Seacoast and Pine Barrens, 1690–1800" (Ph.D. diss. proposal, Rutgers University, 1981), pp. 29–34.

31. Carl Boyer, comp., *Ship Passenger Lists: New York and New Jersey (1600–1825)* (Newhall, Calif.: Carl Boyer, 1978), p. 48; Salter, *A History of Monmouth and Ocean Counties,* p. xxix.

32. Isaac Mickle, *Reminiscences of Old Gloucester* (Philadelphia: Townsent Wart, 1845), p. 85.

33. Revolutionary War Pension and Bounty-Land Warrant Application Files (microfilm), U. S. National Archives, film 27, reel 173.

34. Alfred M. Heston, ed., *South Jersey: A History, 1664–1924* (New York and Chicago: Lewis Historical Publishing Co., 1924), 2: 769n.

35. Blackman, *A History of Little Egg Harbor,* pp. 346–347.

36. *New Jersey Gazette,* August 8, 1781, p. 3.

37. Heston, *South Jersey,* 2: 770, 771; Henry Charlton Beck, "Hanged in Three Places, Buried in Two," *New York Folklore Quarterly* 2 (1947): 242–246.

38. Beck, *Forgotten Towns of Southern New Jersey,* p. 171.

39. Charles F. Green, *Pleasant Mills and Lake Nescochague—A Place of the Olden Days* (N.p., n. d.), pp. 14–15. There is a copy of this work in the Sinclair Collection of the Alexander Library of Rutgers University.

40. Charles J. Peterson, *Kate Aylesford: A Story of the Refugees* (Philadelphia: T. B. Peterson; Boston: Phillips, Sampson and Co.; New York: J. C. Derby, 1855), pp. 50–55.

41. Gustav Kobbe, *The New Jersey Coast and Pines: An Illustrated Guide-book* (Short Hills, N.J.: published by the author, 1889), p. 92.

42. Henry Glassie, *Passing the Time in Ballymenone: Culture and History of an Ulster Community* (Philadelphia: University of Pennsylvania Press, 1982), pp. 124, 126.

43. Fowler, "'Nature Stark Naked,'" pp. 3–6.

44. Glassie, *Passing the Time in Ballymenone,* pp. 650, 746n.

Chapter 4. The "Angel Dancers"

1. Interview, Etta Tice Terhune with David S. Cohen, November 10, 1968.

2. Interview, Emma Mead with David S. Cohen, October 29, 1968.

3. Interview, Susan Terhune and Beulah Terhune English with David S. Cohen, November 10, 1968.

4. *Bergen Index* (Hackensack, N.J.), July 29, 1887.

5. *Bergen Index,* July 15, 1887.

6. Quoted in Theodore Schroeder, " A Unique Case: Unlawful to Get Too Close-Up to God and Jesus," *Truth Seeker* 46 (1920): 170.

7. *Bergen Index,* November 17, 19, 1892.

8. *Bergen Index,* November 22, 1892.

9. Supplement to the *Bergen Index,* May 2, 1893.

10. *Bergen Index,* May 2, 1893.

11. *Bergen Index,* September 16, 1893.

12. *Bergen Index,* October 5, 1893.

13. Ibid.

14. *The Sun* (New York), October 6, 1893.

15. *Bergen Index,* April 4, 1895, p. 3.

16. *The Landscape* (Saddle River, N.J.), quoted in *Bergen Index,* September 23, 1893. For more information about Alfred P. Smith, see David Steven Cohen, "Alfred P. Smith: Bergen County's Latter-Day Ben Franklin," *Journal of the Rutgers University Libraries* 38 (1976): 23–33.

17. *The Landscape,* January 1895, p. 2.

18. Bergen County, Deeds, book 464, pp. 16–20; book 541, pp. 207–209; book 673, pp. 545–547; book 630, pp. 565–570.

19. *Evening Record and Bergen County Herald* (Hackensack, N.J.), January 28, 1905.

20. Bergen County, Deeds, book 752, pp. 144–146; Theodore Schroeder, "Anarchism and 'The Lord's Farm': Record of a Social Experiment," *Open Court* 33 (1919): 600.

21. Theodore Schroeder, "Psychology of One Pantheist," *Psychoanalytic Review* 8 (July 1921): 323.

22. Ibid., pp. 320, 324–325.

23. Ibid., p. 321.

24. Ibid., pp. 321–322.

25. Walter C. Klein, *Johan Conrad Beissel: Mystic and Martinet, 1690–1768* (Philadelphia: University of Pennsylvania Press, 1942), pp. 96, 134, 180.

26. Edward Deming Andrews, *The People Called Shakers: A Search for the Perfect Society,* enl. ed. (New York: Dover, 1953), pp. 90–92.

27. Timothy Dwight, *Travels in New England and New York* (New Haven: published by the author, 1822), 3: 113.

28. Quoted in Andrews, *The People Called Shakers,* pp. 305–306n.

29. Arthur Bestor, *Backwoods Utopias: The Sectarian and Owenite Phases of Communitarian Socialism in America, 1663–1829,* 2d. ed., enl. (Philadelphia: University of Pennsylvania Press, 1970), p. 248.

30. Ibid., p. 251; Robert Fogarty argues that communitarianism continued into the late nineteenth century; see "American Communes, 1865–1914," *Journal of American Studies* 9 (1975): 145–162.

31. Jan Harold Brunvand, *The Vanishing Hitchhiker: American Urban Legends and Their Meaning* (New York: W. W. Norton, 1981); idem, *The Choking Doberman and Other "New" Urban Legends* (New York: W. W. Norton, 1984); idem, *The Mexican Pet: More "New" Urban Legends and Some Old Favorites* (New York: W. W. Norton, 1986); Gary Alan Fine, 'Redemption Rumors: Mercantile Legends and Corporate Beneficence," *Journal of American Folklore* 99 (1986): 208–222; idem, "The Kentucky Fried Rat: Legends and Modern Society," *Journal of the*

Folklore Institute 17 (1980): 222–243; Gary Alan Fine and Ralph L. Rosnow, *Rumor and Gossip: The Social Psychology of Heresay* (New York: Elsevier, 1976).

Chapter 5. Reflections on American Ethnicity

1. Frederick Jackson Turner, "The Significance of the Frontier in American History" (1894), reprinted in *Selected Essays of Frederick Jackson Turner* (Englewood Cliffs, N.J.: Prentice-Hall, 1961), pp. 37–62.

2. Henry Glassie, "The Types of the Southern Mountain Cabin," in Jan Harold Brunvand, *The Study of American Folklore: An Introduction* (New York: W. W. Norton, 1968), pp. 338–370; Glassie and Fred Kniffen, "Building in Wood in the Eastern United States: A Time-Place Perspective," *Geographical Review* 56 (1966): 40–66; Terry G. Jordan and Matti Kaups, *The American Backwoods Frontier: An Ethnic and Ecological Interpretation* (Baltimore and London: Johns Hopkins University Press, 1989); Harold R. Shurtleff, *The Log Cabin Myth* (Gloucester, Mass.: Harvard University Press, 1939); C. A. Weslager, *The Log Cabin in America: From Pioneer Days to the Present* (New Brunswick: Rutgers University Press, 1969).

3. J. Geraint Jenkins, *The English Farm Wagon: Origins and Structure* (Lingfield, England: Oakwood Press, for the Museum of English Rural Life, 1961); John Omwake, *The Conestoga Six-Horse Bell Teams of Eastern Pennsylvania* (Cincinnati: Ebbert and Richardson, 1930); George Schumway and Howard C. Frey, *Conestoga Wagon, 1750–1850; Freight Carrier for One Hundred Years of America's Westward Expansion* (n.p.: George Schumway, 1968).

4. Charles Julian Bishko, "The Peninsular Background of Latin American Cattle Ranching," *Hispanic American Historical Review* 32 (1952): 491–515; Fred Kniffen, "The Western Cattle Complex: Notes

on Differentiation and Diffusion," *Western Folklore* 12 (1953): 179–185; Peter Riviere, *The Forgotten Frontier: Ranchers of Northern Brazil,* Case Studies in Cultural Anthropology (New York: Holt, Rinehart, and Winston, 1972).

5. Andrew W. Crosby, Jr., *The Columbian Exchange: Biological and Cultural Consequences of 1492,* Contributions in American Studies, no. 2 (Westport, Conn.: Greenwood Press, 1972).

6. Ruth Benedict, *Race, Science, and Politics* (New York: Viking Press, 1945), pp. 11–12.

7. Stephen Thernstrom, ed., *Harvard Encyclopedia of American Ethnic Groups* (Cambridge and London: Belknap Press of Harvard University Press, 1980).

8. Robert B. Klymasz, "Ukrainian Folklore in Canada: An Immigrant Complex in Transition (Ph.D. diss., Indiana University, 1971); idem, *Continuity and Change: The Ukrainian Folk Heritage in Canada* (Ottawa: Canadian Centre for Folk Culture Studies, the National Museum of Man, and the National Museums of Canada, 1972); Paul Robert Magocsi, "Ukrainians," in Thernstrom, *Harvard Encyclopedia of American Ethnic Groups,* pp. 200–210; David S. Cohen, *Ukrainian-Americans: An Ethnic Portrait,* photographs by Donald P. Lokuta (Trenton: New Jersey Historical Commission, 1982).

9. Fredrik Barth, ed., *Ethnic Groups and Boundaries* (London and Bergen-Oslo: George Allen and Unwin, Universitets Forlaget, 1969); David Steven Cohen, "How Dutch Were the Dutch in New Netherland?" *New York History* 62 (1981): 43–60; idem, *The Ramapo Mountain People* (1974; reprint, New Brunswick: Rutgers University Press, 1988).

10. *Oxford English Dictionary,* 2d ed. (Oxford: Clarendon Press, 1989), 5: 423–424.

11. W. Lloyd Warner, *Yankee City* (1941–1945; abridged ed., New Haven and London: Yale University Press, 1963), p. 357.

12. John Higham, "Ethnic Pluralism in Modern American

Thought," in *Send These to Me: Immigrants in Urban America,* 2d ed. (Baltimore and London: Johns Hopkins University Press, 1984), pp. 198–232; Jerrold Hirsch, "Portrait of America: The Federal Writers' Project in an Intellectual and Cultural Context" (Ph.D. diss., University of North Carolina, 1984); idem, "Cultural Pluralism and Applied Folklore," in Burt Feintuch, ed., *The Conservation of Culture: Folklorists and the Public Sector* (Lexington: University Press of Kentucky, 1988), pp. 46–67; David Steven Cohen, ed., *America, The Dream of My Life: Selections From the Federal Writers' Project's New Jersey Ethnic Survey* (New Brunswick: Rutgers University Press, 1990), pp. 10–11.

13. Nathan Glazer, *Ethnic Dilemmas, 1964–1982* (Cambridge and London: Harvard University Press, 1983); Howard F. Stein and Robert F. Hill, *The Ethnic Imperative: Examining the New White Ethnic Movement* (University Park and London: Pennsylvania State University Press, 1977); Michael Novak, *The Rise of the Unmeltable Ethnics: Politics and Culture in the Seventies* (New York: Macmillan, 1971); John J. Bukowczyk, *And My Children Did Not Know Me: A History of the Polish-Americans,* Minorities in Modern America (Bloomington: Indiana University Press, 1987), p. 49; Kerby A. Miller, "Class, Culture, and Immigrant Group Identity in the United States: The Case of Irish-American Ethnicity," in Virginia Yans-McLaughlin, ed., *Immigration Reconsidered: History, Sociology, and Politics* (New York and Oxford: Oxford University Press, 1990), pp. 96–129.

14. David Hackett Fischer, *Albion's Seed: Four British Folkways in America* (New York: Oxford University Press, 1990).

15. Thomas J. Archdeacon, *Becoming American: An Ethnic History* (New York and London: Macmillan, 1938), p. 25. These figures computed by Archdeacon are based on estimates in American Council of Learned Societies, "Report of the Committee on Linguistic and National Stocks in the United States," *Annual Report of the American Histor-*

ical Assocation for the Year 1931 (Washington, D.C.: Government Printing Office for the American Historical Association, 1932). These figures have been slightly revised by Thomas L. Purvis, "The European Ancestry of the United States Population, 1790," *William and Mary Quarterly* 41 (1984): 85–135.

16. Leonard Dinnerstein and David M. Reimers, *Ethnic Americans: A History of Immigration and Assimilation* (New York: Dodd, Mead and Co., 1975), pp. 10–55.

17. Bernard Bailyn, *The Peopling of British North America: An Introduction* (New York: Alfred A. Knopf, 1986).

18. Henry F. Dobyns, "Estimating Aboriginal Population: 1. An Appraisal of Techniques with a New Hemispheric Estimate," *Current Anthropology* 7 (1966): 415–416; Cohen, *The Ramapo Mountain People;* "Census Finds Many Claiming New Identity: Indian," *New York Times,* March 5, 1991, pp. A1, A16.

19. Bailyn, *The Peopling of British North America,* pp. 5, 60; James J. Rawley, *The Transatlantic Slave Trade: A History* (New York and London: W. W. Norton, 1981), p. 428.

20. David Ward, *Cities and Immigrants: A Geography of Change in Nineteenth Century America* (New York and London: Oxford University Press, 1971), p. 7; U.S. Bureau of the Census, *Thirteenth Census of the United States, 1910, Population* (Washington, D.C.: Government Printing Office, 1913), 2: 512, 890; 3: 253; U.S. Bureau of the Census, *Historical Statistics of the United States: Colonial Times to 1970* (Washington, D.C.: Government Printing Office, 1975), 1: 139.

21. Computed from figures given in U. S. Immigration and Naturalization Service, *Annual Report* (1973), pp. 53–54; Archdeacon, *Becoming American,* p. 139.

22. "Half of the Nation's Population Lives in Large Metropolitan Areas," *U.S. Department of Commerce News,* February 21, 1991, p. 1.

23. Computed from the U.S. Bureau of the Census, *Historical Statistics,* 1:389–391.

24. U.S. Immigration and Naturalization Service, *Annual Report* (1973), p. 32; U.S. Bureau of the Census, *Statistical Abstract of the United States: 1989* (Washington, D.C.: Government Printing Office, 1989), p. 10; "Census Shows Profound Change in Racial Makeup of the Nation," *New York Times,* March 11, 1991, p. A1.

25. Robert E. Park, Ernest W. Burgess, and Roderick D. McKenzie, *The City* (London: University of Chicago Press, 1967), pp. 9–12, 50–53, 142–155.

26. Humbert S. Nelli, *Italians in Chicago, 1880–1930: A Study in Ethnic Mobility* (New York: Oxford University Press, 1970), pp. 22–54.

27. Raymond Michael Ralph, "From Village to Industrial City: The Urbanization of Newark, New Jersey, 1830–1860" (Ph.D. diss., New York University, 1978), p. 157; U.S. Bureau of the Census, *Thirteenth Census of the United States, 1910. Population* (Washington, D.C.: Government Printing Office, 1913), 3: 152; U.S. Bureau of the Census, *Census of Population and Housing, 1980. Census Tracts. Newark, N.J., SMSA* (Washington, D.C.: Government Printing Office, 1983), pp. P98, P121.

28. William Julius Wilson, *The Truly Disadvantaged: The Inner City, the Underclass, and Public Policy* (Chicago and London: University of Chicago Press, 1987).

29. Ralph, "From Village to Industrial City," p. 157; Clement A. Price, "The Beleaguered City as Promised Land: Blacks in Newark, 1917–1947," in William C. Wright, ed., *Urban New Jersey Since 1870* (Trenton: New Jersey Historical Commission, 1975), pp. 16–17; U.S. Bureau of the Census, *Population and Housing, 1980. Newark SMSA,* pp. P95-P99.

30. U.S. Bureau of the Census, *Fourteenth Census of the United States,* vol. 2, *Population, 1920* (Washington, D.C.: Government Printing Of-

fice, 1922), pp. 738, 745, 747, 1008–1009. It was estimated that 80 percent of New Yorkers born in Lithuania and Russia were Jewish, because of the relatively small number of respondents who listed their native language as Lithuanian or Russian rather than Yiddish or Hebrew.

31. U.S. Senate Immigration Commission, *Immigrants in Industries,* part 24, *Recent Immigrants in Agriculture* (1911), 1: 3–9, 47ff.; 2: 89ff.; Emily Fogg Meade, "The Italian on the Land: A Study of Immigration," U.S. Bureau of Labor, *Bulletin,* no. 70 (1907): 473–533; Dieter Cunz, "Egg Harbor City: New Germany in New Jersey," *Proceedings of the New Jersey Historical Society* 73 (1955): 89–123; Joseph Brandes, *Immigrants to Freedom: Jewish Communities in Rural New Jersey since 1882* (Philadelphia: University of Pennsylvania Press, 1971).

32. Herbert J. Gans, *The Levittowners: Ways of Life and Politics in a New Suburban Community* (New York: Random House, 1967); Will Herberg, *Protestant, Catholic, Jew: An Essay in American Religious Sociology* (1955; reprint, Garden City: Doubleday, 1960).

33. U.S. Bureau of the Census, Municipal Profiles, New Jersey, New Jersey State Library, Trenton, N.J., vol. 9, pt. 1, Belleville Township, pp. P1, P31; vol. 14, pt. 2, South River, pp. P1, P33–35; vol. 15, pt. 4, Spring Lake; U.S. Bureau of the Census, Reappointment/Redistricting Data, New Jersey State Library, Trenton, N.J., pp. 34, 147.

34. Leonard Dinnerstein and Frederic Cople Jaher, *Uncertain Americans: Readings in Ethnic History* (New York: Oxford University Press, 1977), p. 72; U.S. Bureau of the Census, *Statistical Abstract of the United States: 1989,* p. 41.

35. H. L. Mencken, *The American Language: An Inquiry into the Development of English in the United States* (New York: Alfred A. Knopf, 1921), pp. 51–55, 100–109, 197–205.

INDEX

Adamic, Louis, 104
Adams, Elizabeth, 20
advocacy, 6–8, 10
Africa, 6, 34, 35
African Americans, 42, 100, 106,
    116; and American culture, 11,
    115; and ethnicity and race, 102;
    and Native American ancestry, 3,
    20, 21–22, 23, 24, 26, 27; ori-
    gins of, 6, 101–102; and Piney
    ancestry, 55, 57, 58, 59, 61, 62;
    and Ramapo Mountain People
    ancestry, 6, 8, 14, 15, 18, 19–20,
    36, 103; residential segregation
    of, 112–113
Afrocentrism, 11, 105
Afro-Dutch, 21, 42; and African
    survivals, 43–44; creole character
    of, 3, 10, 33; cultural identity of,
    4, 102; folklife of, 45–46; and
    the Ramapo Mountain People,
    18, 19, 36, 103; as a regional
    subculture, 10, 102
Aimwell, Absalom, 40, 41
Albert, Joe and George, 49
Algonquian, 16, 17
America, *see* United States

American Folklife Center, 48
Andrews, Edward Deming, 95
Angel Dancers, 103; and advocacy,
    9–10; charges against, 84–87,
    89; rumors concerning, 5, 78–
    81, 84, 89, 94, 96, 98; at trial,
    87–88, 89–90. *See also* Mnason
anthropology, 6–7
anti-immigration, 11
Ashatama, Elisha Moses, 59, 60
Ash Tamar, 59
Atlantic Monthly, 50, 53

Bailyn, Bernard, 108
Barleton, William, 76
Bates, Benjamin, 67–68
Bates, Widow, 72–74
Beck, Henry Charlton, 55, 56, 62,
    71–72
belief, 9
Bellomont, Lord, 64
Bernard, Francis, 58
Berry, Eliza, 82, 83, 85
Bestor, Arthur, 97
Bible, the, 95, 104; and the Angel
    Dancers, 84, 86, 87, 88, 93

ABOUT THE AUTHOR

avid Steven Cohen is a senior research associate at the New Jersey Historical Commission and the author of several books on New Jersey folklore and history. He has also curated museum exhibitions and produced public television and radio programs about the state.

DATE DUE

			Printed in USA